MODERN MARQUETRY HANDBOOK

Moiree

Lacewood/silky oak

Chinawood

Marquetry Society of America's

MODERN MARQUETRY HANDBOOK

EDITED BY
Harry J. Hobbs and Allan E. Fitchett

THAMES AND HUDSON

Contents

Continued

1. Introduction to marquetry

Marquetry as a method of decorating wood surfaces with colorful thin woods has been in and out of historical records for more than three thousand years. On walls and ceilings of tombs within pyramids the Egyptians painted their methods of sawing and gluing wood. And they left behind in these sanctuaries priceless boxes and furniture enriched with designs composed of colorful woods, gems and precious metals. By current definition their work is called inlay because it involves a recessed area into which small cut pieces of precious wood were inset—inlaid. Also by current definition common in England and in America the term marquetry refers to cut pieces of exotic woods, called veneer, assembled as a design into a single sheet and then glued to a solid surface, usually wood, hardboard or particle board.

Down through the centuries as better methods were devised for cutting wood into thinner sheets of veneer, and better tools were developed for sawing veneers into delicate shapes to compose intricate designs, the practice of marquetry alternately flourished and declined.

When the Roman Empire was rich and powerful precious veneers were imported for use on tables and other furniture. Thuya burl from the Algerian coast was highly prized. Artisans employed by wealthy Romans vied with each other in combining the most prominently figured veneers to create flamboyant marquetry assemblies to lay on cheaper woods. Marquetry examples from the middle ages are scarce. Until the middle of the 16th century when Italian craftsmen revived marquetry as a furniture decorating art, examples of marquetry appear chiefly as decorative panels in the finest European castles and cathedrals.

Invention of the fret saw in the mid-16th century gave marquetry its most efficient veneer-cutting tool. The earliest practical fret saw had a U-shaped metal frame. The open side held a narrow, toothed blade made from clock-spring steel. The frame had enough flex to tighten the blade. Frame saws larger than the fret saw were not new. Clock-spring steel was new and it could be made into a finer-toothed, stronger, narrower blade than ever before. With the fret saw, veneers could be cut more quickly and with greater precision. It is interesting to observe that the fret saw has not changed much in four centuries. It still works on the same mechanical principle and still is one of the primary tools of the marquetarian.

In the late 16th century Andre-Charles Boulle, France's leading cabinetmaker benefiting from the hand-operated fret saw and thinner veneers, became a master of marquetry techniques for furniture decoration. Boulle may have worked with a saw having wood arms. A wood-frame saw called a "Buhl" saw, possibly a copy of Boulle's, was used by early 19th century wood inlayers in Pennsylvania. For designs Boulle drew heavily from famous artists, notably Raphael, Rubens and engraver Stefano della Bella. Boulle's distinctive style spread rapidly to imitators throughout Europe.

Although Leonardo da Vinci in the late 15th century sketched a treadle-operated stationary machine suggesting a jig saw the earliest evidence of a suitable mechanical saw came into use in England in the late 18th century. It was a foot-powered contraption called a "donkey" and was used for cutting marquetry veneers.

The history of art styles and decorative techniques in every medium, marquetry included, reveals ebbing and flowing of popularity. For marquetry the period of here and now is one of vitalized revival. The practice of marquetry as a hobby has been coming on strong for more than a decade in England. This popularity was a major force in the rapid rise of marquetry in America where, since the founding of the Marquetry Society of America in 1972, the art has indeed flourished. Everywhere in America there is an awakened respect for handcrafted work.

The fascination of marquetry starts with admiration of work achieved by others. The compelling appeal is not a desire to own the marquetry picture, the decorated tray, box or table, but to participate in its creation. Americans are naturally creative. Everyone is a doer. And marquetry promises to fulfill the creative instinct, promises to get us doing something with a permanently rewarding result. "If only I could make that beautiful example of marquetry!" Well, you can. That's what this book is all about. It endeavors to show you how. Marquetry Society members have contributed their extensive experience and developed techniques in everything from selecting appropriate veneers to cutting, assembling and finishing marquetry designs. Here you find modern methods being followed by today's marquetarians.

The beginner can practice marquetry on the kitchen table with a simple, inexpensive assortment of tools and materials that can be brought to the table in a cardboard box. The chapter on tools and equipment calls out the first essentials and also shows additional things you will want as confidence rises with improving skills.

A marquetry project starts with a paper pattern of a pictorial subject or design. The pattern provides cutting outlines for the veneer parts needed to express the design. Although the versatile fret saw is a highly dependable tool for this purpose, preferred by many experienced users, the primary tool to start with is a craft knife so sharp that it can cut thin wood with surprising precision. The thin wood, called veneer, comes in thicknesses of 1/40" to 1/28" and in a multiplicity of colors and intriguing figurations. Cut parts are put together to form the design, and the resulting assembly is glued to a solid surface. What you make in this manner can be a picture for wall decoration or a design to be laid on a table top, cabinet panel, drawer front or any other appropriate surface. Examples of modern marquetry creations are displayed in the following chapter to show what has been made by others who once were beginners, some of them beginners not so long ago.

Since 1927 this classic jig saw, pedal-powered, rocker arm principle, has been cutting veneer for marquetry pictures. Owned and used all this time by David E. Doudna. Photograph by member Bruce C. Kent. By 1929 motorized jig saws, mass produced at six dollars to meet the demand of home shop jigsaw puzzlers, gave the marquetry pad-cutting method new popular appeal.

2. Modern marquetry examples—pictorial and applied

A marquetry assembly is a sheet of veneer composed of cut parts fitted together into a design. This sheet is sometimes called a lay-on because it must be glued to a stable, solid surface. An assembly of veneer parts is never sturdy enough to be used free-standing. The choice of surface, or the end use of your marquetry assembly, stretches just about as far as your ingenuity and current level of skill. Marquetarians, thinking in terms of usage, are accustomed to classify marquetry as either pictorial or applied. Pictorial in this sense refers to pictures to be hung on a wall. Applied refers to marquetry assemblies laid on table tops, chest drawer fronts, cabinet panels and other objects of use. The subject matter of the lay-on is not taken into account in making this separation of usage. Obviously a pictorial subject becomes a piece of applied marquetry when laid on a serving tray. And a non-pictorial geometric or cubistic design becomes a picture when used as a wall hanging. In this chapter the two classes of marquetry assemblies are divided as far as possible into categories signifying usage.

Pictorial. The assembly of illustrated pictures represents a sampling of modern techniques used by contributing Society mem-

Harry Jason Hobbs

Allan E. Fitchett

9

bers to create pictures in a wide assortment of subjects. Where known, title and maker are credited. Shown first are two picture plaques which represent very simple marquetry techniques. Only two kinds of veneer were used for the cocker spaniels shown in silhouette. The dogs were cut from dyed wood and used as templates for defining the two windows required in the one-piece limba background. The second example of simplified marquetry is a picture representing a bighorn sheep standing majestically on a rocky precipice. This is truly a beginner's project that looks much more difficult than it is. To reproduce a picture essentially like this, with a single dominating animal figure, a fret saw is used for cutting a pad of three contrasting veneer sheets in such a way that the pad yields three background pieces that fit together perfectly. A craft knife or a fret saw is used to cut the bighorn sheep separately. It then serves as a template for scribing and cutting a window for insetting bighorn into the background. Other illustrated marquetry examples in this extensive picture gallery were produced by techniques, both simple and advanced, which are explained throughout the book. This sampling of both simple and advanced work is intended to encourage the beginner and to challenge the master.

The First Christmas/Jerry Sprankel design
made by Allan E. Fitchett

Aleck H. Gordon

Peter L. Rose

Peter L. Rose

11

Robert J. Witkowski

Carl F. Grunwald

Charles Kidger

John G. Fielitz

William Profet

John Jordan

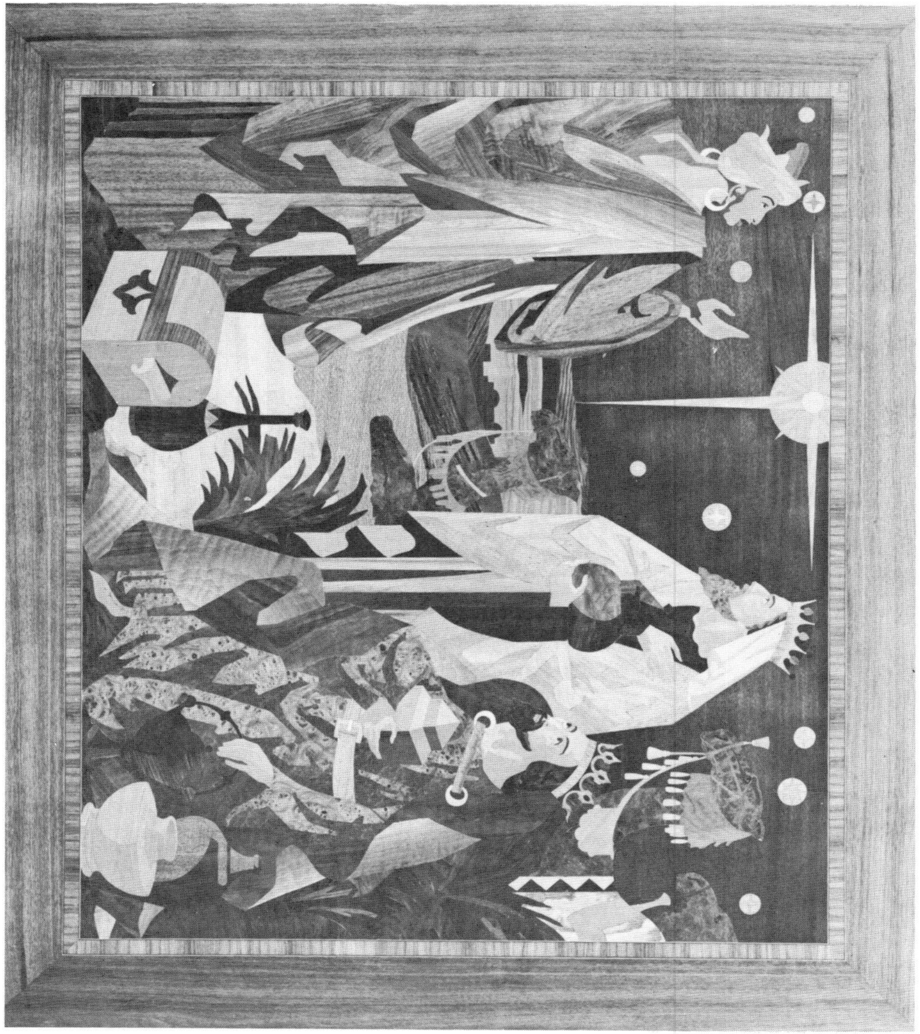

John Jordan

The Three Wisemen

Albert C. Parker

Spring Flowers

Peter L. Rose

14

John G. Fielitz

Cape Cod Street

Egyptian Water Bearer/Jerry Sprankel design
made by Allan E. Fitchett

J. Dale

Albert C. Parker

15

James Belmonte

Logging In Winter

James Belmonte

Peter L. Rose

16

Applied marquetry. Throughout its long history, whenever marquetry appeared it was used predominantly for the embellishment of fine furniture and for insets into wall paneling and cabinets. The most abundant examples are seen in tables of all kinds. The present revival of the art of marquetry, as viewed by many marquetarians, is directed once again toward the enrichment of furniture and other useful objects for the home. Only a small sampling of many popular applications is shown but the range of projects being produced is impressive. Illustrated subjects include serving trays, butler tables, muffin stand, tilt-top occasional table and a walnut tray which was inlaid with veneer and brass. Other possibilities are limited only by available working time and the practicality of the project. Appropriate applications include clock cases, boxes, desk sets, logos, nameplates, lamp bases, cabinet doors, headboards, chest fronts, gameboards and even car dash panels.

One of the simplest forms of applied marquetry, and a good project for the beginner, is decoration for the universally popular small gift box. The easiest approach is to veneer all sides without design of any kind and to make a marquetry lay-on for the lid. Serving trays can start with a panel of plywood or hardboard. Guard against the use of a panel too heavy for a small tray.

Veneer panel edges. Lay your marquetry assembly on top. Veneer the back for balanced construction to offset any tendency to warp. A gallery around the tray is optional. Small blocks glued underneath can eliminate handles. By adding legs to a similar tray you can make a beautiful chair-side table. Various styles of hardware are available for attaching legs to a table top. You can make your own clock. Start with a square or circular panel. Make a marquetry assembly for the face. Attach brass numerals. Install a battery clock movement on the back. Make initialed desk-set boxes. Build a simple gametable and lay a marquetry chess or backgammon face on the panel serving as the top. Custom jewelry, another possibility for marquetry, offers a use for veneer leftovers and could turn into a spare-time source of profit. Small pieces of purpleheart, rosewood or padauk make excellent backgrounds for initials or a tiny silhouette. Sandwich and cement a small veneer assembly between two 1/16" sheets of clear acrylic. Drill a hole for a pendant chain. Visits to museums, gift shops and furniture stores are almost certain to suggest a long list for future projects. The periodic News Letter sent to members of the Marquetry Society is another constant source for ideas and guidance. Ideas will seek you out, and projects will fill your leisure hours to overflowing when you become a marquetarian.

Harold Wasserman

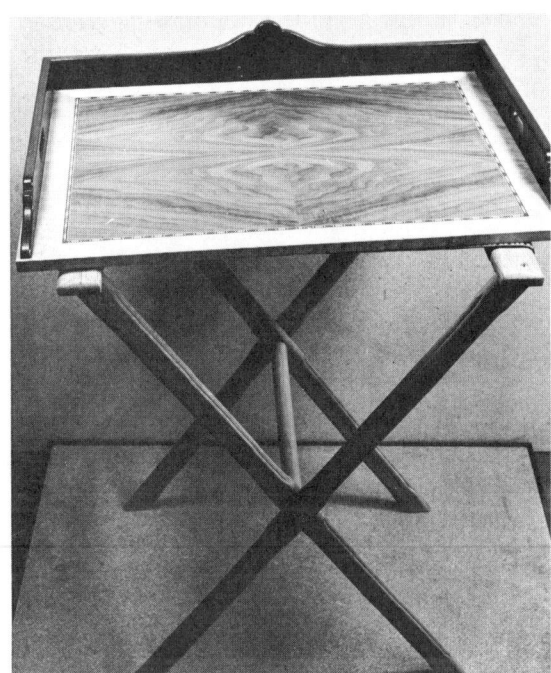

Allan E. Fitchett

19

3. Selecting designs and creating patterns

The first essential in marquetry is an ink drawing of the subject you intend to reproduce in wood. This type of drawing is called a pattern and it must be the same size as the project you are going to make. You can obtain a pattern by purchasing a kit of marquetry materials from a wide variety of subjects offered by suppliers, or you can develop your own patterns. After you have been involved with marquetry for a short time you inevitably start looking at outstanding paintings and photographs from a new viewpoint. "Can I make it in wood?"

Many pictures are too detailed for marquetry. But there must be thousands accessible to you in libraries, museums, magazines and in your own collection of prints and slides that could be simplified and interpreted for your marquetry masterpiece. Select subjects you like and then study your choices to determine which ones can be adapted to your present level of skill.

When you examine a subject which you wish to convert to a marquetry pattern it is important to remember that your palette of veneers is far more restricted than the painter's mix of pigments. The predominating color in your assortment of natural veneers is brown. The range of tints and shades of brown, fortunately, reaches from very light tan to almost black. Within this range there are mixes of yellow tans and yellow browns, as well as reddish tans and reddish browns. And there are brownish reds. Of course there are dyed woods in a wide spectrum of colors, but they are used with restraint. Natural woods are indeed colorful, but when designing for marquetry you should keep sharply in mind the color range you have to work with to achieve essential contrast between one picture element and its neighbor. Color and figure contrast are vital.

Carefully study the picture you wish to reproduce in wood. Is there a story idea or a

3-1. Best photo subjects have single dominating element. Sailboat has action and composition

3-2. Floral displays can be difficult, but this one has well-defined outlines suitable to veneer

20

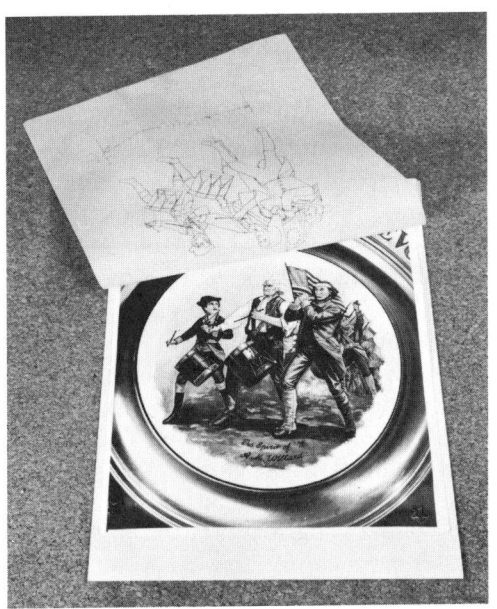

3-3. To convert photo into marquetry pattern lay tracing paper over photo. Trace main outlines

3-4. Photo tracing is enlarged to desired size. Each area enclosed by lines represents veneer

mood that would be extremely difficult to express within the formal pattern lines and tonal limitations of wood? Or is there a dominating element that can be interpreted unmistakably in wood?

For example, a single sailboat (3-1) caught by the camera at a dramatic moment qualifies for simplicity and artistic composition. A floral display of chrysanthemums (3-2) arranged in a group of well-defined outlines qualifies for depiction in wood. These flower petals have crisp, formal outlines and each can be separated from the mass by the simple trick of providing color contrast. Color variety is a natural ingredient in a floral display and is easily fulfilled by a combination of natural and dyed woods.

Now and then from strange places come good subjects. A souvenir bicentennial serving plate provided the original design for the "Spirit of '76." A photograph of the plate is used as the original for one of the following patternmaking demonstrations.

It is safe to assume that many marquetarians are not artists with the ability to pick up a pen and create a line drawing. The common problem for most of us non-artists is how to convert a painting, photograph, or even a textile design into an ink line drawing. There are several ways of making this conversion from original picture to pattern.

Direct tracing. From an art supplies store procure a pad of translucent tracing paper or a sheet of mat acetate. Lay a sheet over the picture. (3-3) Hinge the tracing sheet to the picture by taping it along the upper edge. You will want to lift it frequently for inspection of detail in the original as tracing progresses. Using a fine-point dark pencil, No. 1 preferred, trace the outlines of essen-

3-5. Veneers chosen for color and figure create remarkably good depiction of colorful subjects

tial elements. Dark lead makes a prominent line without leaving a pressure imprint on the original.

The confusion of elements in the background of "Spirit of '76" will be omitted. Only the two drummers, the fife player and the flag are necessary to the scene. Remember that every line you draw represents the edge of a piece of veneer which must be cut with knife or saw.

For a lesson in simplification compare the line drawing with the photograph (3-4) to see how the drum, clothing, hands and other details can be adequately shown by a small number of single pieces. Examine the coat sleeve and the trousers of the fife player; one piece of veneer for each element. Notice how a change of color contrast is achieved where the coat tail lining is exposed and is interrupted by one trouser leg. This patternmaking technique of interruption makes both neighboring elements clearly defined and readily recognized. This is a useful technique as you can see in the finished plaque. (3-5)

Every line you draw must meet another line to form an island. Every island must be cut from veneer. Later on you will learn tricks in shading that will provide another way to create contrast, but in the beginning you should make a complete outline, an island, for every color.

Remove tracing paper from the original and fill in any worthwhile additions or take out any details. Keep in mind that the pattern will come alive when colorful woods

take the place of blank outlines. And interesting figures of the woods you select will add visual texture to the various elements.

Indirect tracing. When dark details in the original picture cannot be seen clearly through tracing paper or acetate, here is a way to solve the problem. Forget the tracing paper. Tape a piece of white paper under the original picture. Slip a sheet of carbon paper between the original and the paper. Lay this assembly on a smooth, flat surface and proceed to trace the main outlines of the original with a stylus. (3-6) Draw lightly to avoid a pressure imprint on the original. You can go over the carbon image to heavy it after removing the original. To convert this indirect tracing into a pattern lay tracing paper over it and prepare an ink drawing.

Lightbox tracing. If you are going to do much tracing it could be worth your time to construct a simplified version of the lightbox used in camera stores for viewing negatives. Make yours larger to accommodate work patterns. You need nothing more than a four-sided box with a sheet of frosted glass on top and a light bulb inside. A bottom is not essential, but air vents in the sides are needed. In use you tape the original to glass

3-6. Indirect tracing of original picture using stylus, carbon paper and sheet of white paper

3-7. Lightbox provides one of the best ways to follow details in original subject for tracing

22

and tape tracing paper over the original. With the light turned on, you can readily see through the original. (3-7) In this procedure it is good practice to draw an initial outline lightly. When satisfied with results go over all lines with a black ballpoint pen or with a drafting pen and India ink. Use an art gum eraser to remove pencil marks after the ink has dried.

Mechanical aids. Modern photographic equipment offers a definite advantage in creating line drawings for marquetry. Suitable equipment can project a picture to create an enlarged or reduced image for tracing. This time-saving one-step procedure can be carried out on any of three types of equipment which you may already own.

Opaque projector. If you own or can borrow an opaque projector just mount your picture in the copy holder, turn on the built-in light and project the image onto white paper taped to a vertical surface in front of the machine. The size you project is regulated by moving the projector closer or farther from the paper. Trace the image.

Slide projector. The same projector you use for showing your color slides can be enlisted for pattern work. It will be necessary to take a photograph of the original picture. The color slide or black-and-white negative can be put into the machine and projected to required size onto white paper to create a traceable image. (3-8)

Photo enlarger. Again you need a negative. Place it in the negative holder on the machine and project the image onto white paper on the table.

Pantograph. A drawing instrument known as a pantograph is a handy device for producing enlarged or reduced copies of original drawings. It consists of four wood or metal arms connected together in parallelogram fashion to which are affixed a stylus and a writing head.

To get the most out of the pantograph mount it on a drafting table or similar smooth surface. (3-9) Mount it approximately eight inches up from the lower left-hand corner of the work surface near the left edge. The mounting location and depth of the work surface should be such that the pantograph does not hang up by dropping off the rear edge.

Pick a major dimension of the item to be copied and measure its length. Determine the length you want for this dimension in the final drawing. Divide the larger number by the smaller to get the magnification factor. To illustrate, assume the original is a picture of a house that is four inches across the front. You decide that the resulting drawing is to

3-8. Photo slide projector casts enlarged image of photo negative. Image easily traced on paper

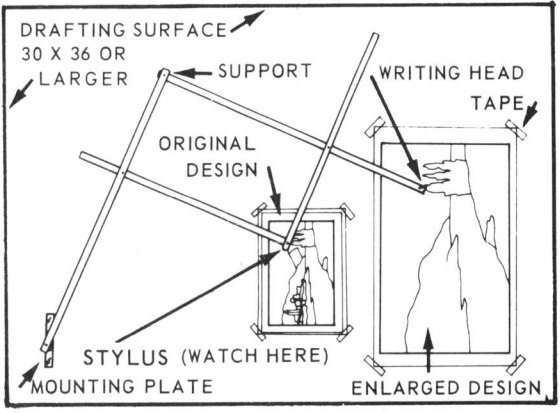

3-9. Pantograph is mechanical means of enlarging or reducing original pictures or drawings

contain the house with a dimension of ten inches across. Ten inches divided by four inches gives a magnification factor of two and one half.

The pantograph is adjusted by removing the adjustable pivots, aligning the arms so that they cross at the holes marked with the desired magnification and reinserting the pivots. Since the pantograph is not continuously adjustable it may be necessary to pick an available magnification factor nearest to that calculated. Enlargement or reduction for an end product is determined by interchanging the locations of the writing head with the stylus. Enlargement occurs when the writing head is mounted on the right-most arm of the pantograph.

Extend the pantograph to the right across the work surface so that the stylus and writing head are in conveniently spaced locations. This will generally occur when the arms form a rectangle. This also tends to be the most accurate position of the pantograph. Slide the original under the stylus and locate it so that the stylus rests on the center. Do this without moving the pantograph. Slide the paper on which the copy is to be made under the writing head in a similar manner. Temporarily hold original and copy paper in place with masking tape.

Some adjustment in paper location will be required to obtain the final alignment. At this time manipulate the pantograph to place the stylus at the left margin of the original. Then check to see if the writing head is at the left margin of the copy paper. The right margin positions are checked in the same manner, and the paper is relocated according to the drawing requirements.

The whole procedure is repeated for the upper and lower margins. The paper is shifted to its final position and secured with masking tape. Care must be exercised in locating original and copy paper to insure that they do not overlap or run off the edge of the work surface.

The best lead used in the writing head of the pantograph is a 2H grade lead. It gives sufficiently dark lines while being hard enough to require infrequent sharpening.

With one hand on the writing head and the other on the stylus, the stylus is maneuvered over the lines of the original. Manipulation comes from experience and will differ according to personal preference. (3-10)

Always look at the stylus when tracing the lines of the original. With a little practice it will become automatic to apply light pressure to the writing head while tracing lines and to lift it between lines. This will be true even though you never look away from the stylus while the pantograph is in motion. Plenty of light helps in accurately following the lines.

If straight lines are essential in the finished product one technique which gives excellent results is to mark the ends of the lines with the pantograph. Then use a straightedge to draw between the located end points. Do only a few lines at a time so as to keep your place on the pattern of resulting dots.

All copying of this type requires touch-up. For this purpose suitable erasers, erasing shields and pencils should be available. Good, dark, final copy may be produced by tracing over the resulting drawing with a fine felt-tipped pen.

Grids. If you have no other means of enlarging a drawing you can resort to the familiar system of grids or graph squares. The basic principle requires small squares on the line drawing you have created and larger squares on a sheet of paper for developing an enlarged image. On one copy of your line drawing (always keep a spare copy) draw ink or pencil lines accurately spaced 1/4" apart. Key the vertical lines alphabetically and the horizontal lines numerically. (3-11)

You can enlarge in any ratio, but assuming an enlargement of double size take a piece of white paper at least twice the size of the original and draw 1/2" squares. Again number and letter the lines. Observe where each design line crosses a graph line on the original. Locate this point on the enlarged graph. Make a dot. Continue to locate intersecting points. Eventually you can start to connect the marked points while you constantly refer to the original in order to duplicate the direction of the design line within each squared-off area. (3-12) Connecting the points requires a bit of freehand drawing to maintain the curving lines of the original, but this is a fairly easy exercise. Now you have a twice-size pattern drawing ready for final inking. With a little experience you will reduce some of the pointing off. If you want an easier, faster system you can work with printed acetate grid sheets sold at some art supplies stores. Simply lay the grid sheet over your original line drawing, tape it in place and then develop only the graph squares needed for the enlargement. This is an excellent system when you prefer not to deface your original.

Mechanical enlargements. The simplest and most accurate enlargement or reduction of your line pattern is a photostat. This is a two-step process normally, but you can buy just the first step which gives you a white line on black paper for tracing by yourself. Or you can also buy the second step which is a positive, black line on white paper. A newer version of this mechanical process is called a PMT print. This is a one-step process which gives you whatever new size of pattern you require, black line on white paper.

Reversing a drawing. Some marquetry cutting techniques require a pattern in reverse. If you were working from a photo negative or slide you could simply have reversed it in the machine so that a reverse image was projected for tracing. If, however, your pattern drawing is now complete and you find that you want it reversed, slip a piece of carbon paper under the pattern, carbon side facing the pattern, and trace the pattern itself with a stylus. The reverse image is transferred to the back side of the pattern and is ready for duplicating. If you prefer not to mark the back of the pattern lay a piece of white paper between pattern and carbon.

If you are going to add inlay strips and borders to your wood picture add these features to your line drawing so that your pattern is complete.

Duplicate copying. It is always desirable to make duplicate copies of your completed line drawing. You may use one copy for a working pattern, you may sometime share

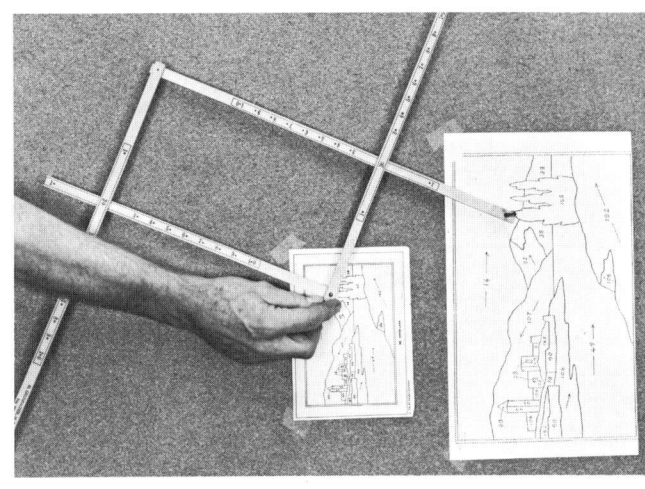

3-10. When stylus is moved around small drawing the writing head reproduces enlarged image

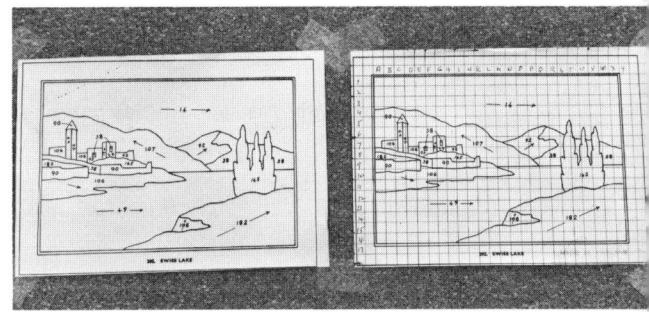

3-11. Left, original drawing. Right, on duplicate draw graph squares. Assign numbers and letters

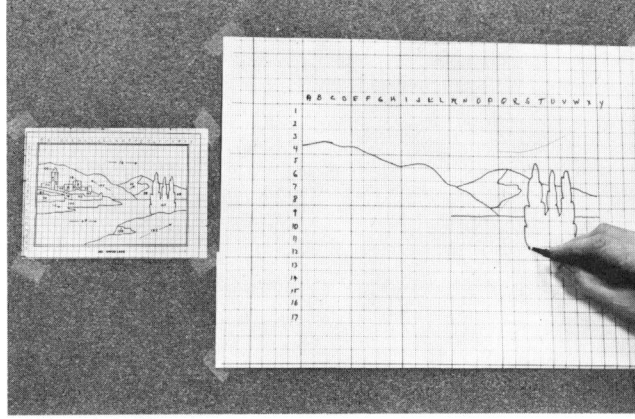

3-12. To enlarge a drawing prepare large graph and make dots at keyed locations. Connect dots

25

your creation with others, or you may decide to start your own pattern library. It is wise not to use your one and only copy as a working pattern which will ultimately be cut up and destroyed in the cutting process. Furthermore you need one extra copy for reference as you work.

Duplicate copies are easily obtained from today's duplicating equipment, especially from photocopy machines. If your original pattern is too large for the duplicating machine make copies in sections and then tape the sections together. Photostat and blueprint concerns have equipment for duplicating practically any size drawing. If you buy a negative photostat of final size you can then use it to make photocopies, or you can trace as many copies as you need, using tracing paper or white paper interleaved with carbon paper.

Pattern breakup. Some complex subjects involving intricate or large, delicate elements are more safely handled if the subject is broken into sections. The Fitchett coat of arms shown is a good example.

The marquetry reproduction of the coat of arms started with a printed copy. (3-13) A line drawing of a photo enlargement was prepared. Sections were divided for size and ease in handling.

3-13. Enlarged line drawing of coat of arms was broken into manageable sections for cutting

Shield—contains large lion and band
Band—cuts diagonally through shield
Mantle—surrounds top and sides
Torse—wreath on top of helmet
Helm—aluminum helmet
Crest—brass lion on top of helmet
Motto—scroll containing name

Each section was developed as a separate piece of marquetry. All cutting was done on a power scroll saw using No. 4/0 blade. When all sections were complete each was carefully cut into a walnut background. When everything was in place the entire veneer assembly was contact-cemented to a 3/4" particle board panel. Edges and back were veneered. The completed plaque was scraped, sanded and varnished.

26

"Egyptian Water Bearer" is example of how marquetry pattern was developed from art source. Original painting was found on the wall of an ancient tomb. Pyramids added to pattern relate subject to Egypt

Make your selection of veneers for this pattern—a modern interpretation of "The First Christmas"

4. Veneers — kinds, characteristics and selection

Your enjoyment of marquetry as a hobby will be greatly intensified by a basic knowledge of woods. There are many interesting, comprehensive books available to you in libraries for borrowing, in local bookstores, and specialty catalogs for ordering. (*See Bibliography*)

You can indulge your leisure time happily in marquetry, however, without knowing correctly whether the veneer you are using was sliced from a half-log, a full-log flitch or was rotary cut on a lathe. This observation is not to minimize frivolously the value of having a thorough understanding of your medium. It is intended to get you started in the practice and enjoyment of marquetry without delay.

You can study the basics of wood as you go along. You can trace the country of origin, the botanical names, variations of common names throughout the world, and manufacturing methods for the veneers you are working with. You can discover how different manufacturing methods can produce anything from plain to fancy figuration from the same log. Meanwhile, as an introduction some of the more useful essentials of background are covered here.

Hardwood trees. There are two botanical classes of wood. Trees with broad leaves yield hardwoods. Trees having needlelike or scalelike leaves, most of which are evergreen, yield softwoods. The terms are not wholly descriptive. Although most hardwoods are hard, strong-grained and dense, many are no harder than some softwoods. Nevertheless our concern in marquetry is with the hardwoods. They are the most colorful and the most pleasantly figured. Hardwoods are the most workable; they cut best with knife and saw; they splinter the least; they take a better finish than softwoods; and they look more beautiful. They are the choice veneers used in marquetry.

The above descriptions apply to the botanical classifications of trees and the woods they yield. In that sense the terms are written as one word, hardwood or softwood. Marquetarians, while stockpiling hardwoods, are thinking only in terms of working properties of those woods. They apply their own terminology of hard wood meaning hard surface, dense, strong; or soft wood meaning soft surface, easily indented and easily cut with a craft knife. In botanical terms mahogany is a hardwood, but it has a relatively soft texture and cuts easily with a craft knife, so marquetarians consider mahogany as a soft wood.

Veneer width. Your primary material for marquetry is veneer. Veneer is thin wood. Veneers are sliced from hardwood trees that may have been growing for 100 to 120 years in lush tropical forests in foreign lands. Unimagined hardships surround the harvesting of trees like teak, as an example. Deep in thick jungle forests of Burma, teak trees standing nearly 100 feet tall are so heavy that they are girdle-cut and left to stand for three years to dry before they are light enough to cut, haul to waterways and float to coastal ports for export.

A log of African mahogany harvested along the Ivory Coast will measure 3 to 6 feet in diameter and may yield a usable trunk as long as 90 feet. A large commercially valuable tree you may know is the American sycamore which grows in the eastern part of the central and southern plains. Heights reach 120 feet. Sycamores yield plentiful quantities of veneer which you will find highly useful because of width.

The size of hardwood trees is of special significance in marquetry. Large trees yield wide veneers. You will be grateful for wide veneers when planning the large areas of a picture like sky, mountain and plain. Wide sheets again are a big convenience when you look in your stockpile for a single sheet wide enough to make a one-piece backing veneer for a mounting panel.

Depending upon current availability, veneers in widths of more than 12" include the mahogany family, sycamore, butternut, teak, and maple. Other veneers come in widths of 6" to 12". Macassar ebony, tamo ash, lacewood, padauk, tulipwood, English oak, satinwood, and pearwood generally are narrow, some only 3½" to 5" wide. In practice the narrow widths seldom become a handicap because most of the individual elements you cut for a picture are smaller than available veneer widths. Length is no factor at all. The standard in the hobby market is 3-foot lengths for all kinds except for burls, butts and crotches.

Veneer thickness. There is no longer a standard thickness of veneer. Until recent years most veneers in the hobby market were 1/28", 0.9 mm. Now many of the important kinds are produced only in the thinner form of 1/40", 0.7 mm. (4-1) The two thicknesses present a problem to the marquetarian, but

_____

4-1. Comparative thickness of most veneers now offered. Top line 1/28 in. Bottom line 1/40 in.

watchfulness when procuring veneers can largely overcome the problem. Two thicknesses of veneer in the same picture can be brought to a common level by sanding after assembly. But it is somewhat simpler to re-

strict your selection of veneers to either 1/28" or 1/40" in a given assembly. Electing to work with one thickness, of course, limits your freedom of selection. In time you will develop a working procedure that will minimize the difference or ignore the difference until time for sanding. One such procedure is to laminate two thicknesses of the thinner veneer. This piece is then slightly thicker than the 1/28" which may surround it, but the raised piece is readily reduced by using a scraper on the side to be glued to a panel. Or level it by sanding.

Dyed veneers. You can now buy better dyed veneers from American suppliers than those imported a few years ago. The new offerings have more wood figure. They are more stable and are dyed uniformly through the wood so they can be sanded without fading. Woods used in dyeing are sycamore, birch, maple and aspen. They retain mild figurations and look like real wood, which they are.

There are two thicknesses, 1/28" and 1/40". This factor enables you to match dyed veneer thickness with natural veneer thickness. The 1/40" is easier to knife-cut.

Colors of the woods range from very subtle, subdued colors to brilliant colors. One supplier offers 24 colors in each thickness. There are pinks, reds, yellow, blue, purple, black, tangerine and more. One called Gulf Stream green creates a pleasing imitation of calm water in pond, lake or stream. There is an emerald green for bright leaves. Olive green and tropic green make darker leaves. Bird's-eye maple, bleached white, is very appealing. It is whiter than holly.

Dyed woods in marquetry are surrounded with opinion. Some craftworkers advocate only natural woods. Others believe that colored woods are essential to simulate birds, flowers, costumes, heraldry crests, logos and trademarks.

Wood identification is the most useful essential in your study of woods. When you are ordering veneers from a mail-order supplier, as most of us do, you need to know what to order besides maple, walnut and mahogany. The more woods you can distinguish in a long list of available veneers, the better your pictures. Exotic woods make the best pictures and marquetry designs.

What is benge? What is bubinga? Eucalyptus? Koa? Lacewood? Satinwood? Moiree? Tola?

It is extremely important to develop an early knowledge of wood figure. No two woods have the same figuration, and woods of the same species can vary markedly depending on which part of the tree they come from and how they are cut.

Figure is the design pattern you see in wood. That is not the grain. In a sheet of flat-cut walnut the grain runs straight, but the figure is a series of converging diamonds. A sheet of curly maple has subdued straight grain running east and west. But the beautiful, lustrous figure that attracts your attention is a series of closely formed wavy brush strokes, alternating shadow and highlight, running north and south. Because many popular woods are light brown, and many medium brown, figure sometimes becomes the best key to identifying wood.

A few examples will illustrate the importance of learning to identify woods so that you can visualize their appearance when you see the name. For instance, one catalog offering veneers for marquetry includes "satinwood, straight stripe" and "satinwood, bee's-wing." What does bee's-wing look like? What could it represent? The color is a strong yellow gold. The figure is a composite of small spots of gold burnished into short brush strokes that could readily suggest the yellow leaves of a birch tree or ash in an autumn scene.

Prima vera and avodire are pale gold. At a glance they look somewhat alike. But avodire has more figure, subtle and wavy. It would make a more interesting sky than prima vera.

Is the figure pattern of "teak, figured" large or small figured? Generally it is large, too large to represent small details. Small figuration—delicate little flecks, swirls and lines—are generally more useful in pictorial marquetry.

You need to know at least a dozen or more woods by color and figure in order to procure an assortment to get you started. Unless, of course, you first work with a complete marquetry kit.

In this chapter we include a collection of wood-grain photographs which give you a start in identification on the basis of figure. An even better introduction to popular veneers for marquetry is available in a box of 4" x 9" sample woods. One box contains 40 kinds, another 50 kinds. All are identified for study and reference.

Working characteristics. It is helpful to know the cutting quality of veneers that appeal to you in color and figure. Without having veneers on hand for inspection, you may be glad for suggested good choices. Saw-cutting methods can handle almost any kind of veneer. Even the unruly kinds become manageable with special techniques such as the protective saw pad. Beginners at knife-cutting, however, will find some veneers too hard, too brittle or too crumbly for easy cutting. But there are many woods that respond very well to knife-cutting.

Woods for easy knife-cutting

avodire	mahogany
benge	pearwood
birch	peroba
butternut	poplar
cherry	poplar burl
gumwood	sapele
harewood	sycamore
holly	walnut

Not so easy knife-cutting

Brazilian rosewood	padauk
bubinga	redwood burl
ebony	satinwood
English oak	tamo ash
eucalyptus	teak
lacewood	thuya burl
olive ash	zebrano

Selection. When you are ready to select veneers for a picture select first for color, second for figure, third for contrast. Decide on color values appropriate to the scene. Then start your selection with veneers for the large areas of background. With woods you do not have the freedom or range of color and texture allowed the painter. No blue veneers for a sky, for instance. What you select for sky, mountain, field and water will come from a range of pale yellow, gold, gray, tan, many shades of brown, and some of these shades will be faintly washed with tints of pink, green, orange, purple. Your job is to choose veneer that simulates the object, both in color and pattern. Don't try too hard to be realistic. No round disc of red veneer can reproduce a many-toned setting sun. Veneer can only create the impression of a sunset. When surrounded by other elements like a chinawood sky and a low gumwood mountain, the red disc dropping behind the mountain is unmistakably the setting sun.

The success of your depiction of the scene rests largely with your artistic judgment. That is what selection comes down to — your ability to blend an assortment of colors and patterns into a pleasing, harmonious, meaningful scene. Each person's interpretation will be different. The New Englander and the Texan have different color values of sky, mountain, field and foliage.

To illustrate the principles of selection a list of elements frequently found in pictures was compiled. Several marquetarians were asked to suggest a few appropriate woods. When studying the list keep in mind that season and time of day expressed in a picture can influence the choices you make. Of course there are many other suitable woods for each element, but this list could make it easier for you to get started.

Picture elements and appropriate woods

Barns: Oriental wood, sapele, walnut, Sunset Red

Boulders: walnut burl, Carpathian elm burl, thuya burl

Fields: oak, butternut, peroba

Flesh tones: pearwood, birch, sycamore

Floral subjects: satinwood, avodire, purpleheart, madrone, cherry, cedar

Mountains: gumwood, paldao, kelobra, Brazilian rosewood, teak

Roofs: zebrano, lacewood, East Indian rosewood, mahogany mottle

Sandy beaches: sycamore, birch, oak, butternut

Shadows: walnut, harewood

Sky: ash, avodire, aspen, sycamore, birch, gumwood, chinawood, cedar

Snow: holly, beech

Stonework: harewood, eucalyptus, lacewood, birch, English oak

Streets: pecan, oak

Trees and bushes: walnut butts and burls, poplar burl, mahogany mottle, madrone, redwood burl, avodire, olive ash, satinwood bee's-wing

Water: Gulf Stream Green, Tropic Green, harewood, sycamore

Wood siding: striped narra, padauk, Honduras mahogany, benge

Wooden fences: any narrow-striped veneer selected for color contrast

Wood color chart. With more than a hundred woods available it is a formidable mental project to memorize the ranges of color, figure and texture. Favorites, because easily recalled, are often used where a lesser known wood could greatly improve the desired effect. A handy visual aid is needed.

The most helpful aid in selection is a collection of wood samples mounted on a panel. With color arranged in groups as on the color chart suggested here (4-2) a comprehensive range of reds, for example, can be examined and compared quickly.

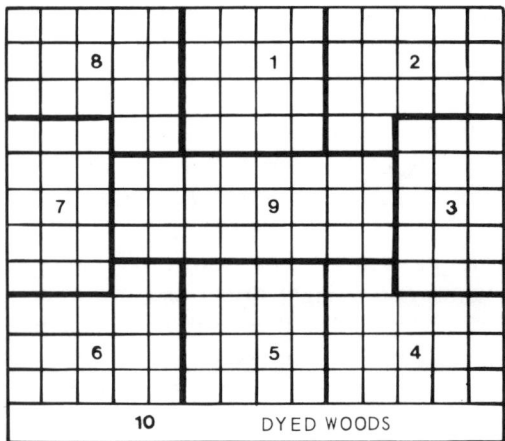

4-2. Chart design for mounting veneer samples according to color as a quick aid to selection

This model chart was made with 1" veneer samples mounted on a panel slightly over 15" wide and 12" deep. It displays about 125 woods and has spaces for additions. Samples 2" square, while doubling the panel size, would provide a more typical representation of each wood.

Visualized as a clock, the chart starts with the lightest woods in Area 1 at 12 o'clock and moves around to the darkest woods in Area 5

32

at 6 o'clock. Area 9 at the center displays special effect woods such as butts, burls, crotches and swirls. Each wood is labeled beneath the sample and coded to supplier.

The following assignment to color categories was made from one marquetarian's collection of samples. Another person's collection most likely includes lighter or darker specimens that dictate a shift from one area to another. Assignment becomes an individual problem.

AREA 1 Lightest shades

holly	harewood (white)	ramin
poplar	white maple	ash
pine	aspen	quaking aspen
tupelo	white birch	abele

AREA 2 Whites to light pinks

red birch	bird's-eye maple	elm
pearwood	red oak	cherry
cedar	beech	apple
pecan	yew	gaboon

AREA 3 Dark pinks to reds

Honduras mahogany	padauk	eucalyptus
mahogany stripe	kevazingo	sapele
tulipwood	koa	almondwood
lacewood	red cedar	makore, pink

AREA 4 Dark reds to darkest reds

African cherry	bubinga	kelobra
purpleheart	utile	ramon
rosewood (S. Dom.)	Afr. mahog.	rosewood (E. Ind.)
jarrah	acacia	mahogany crotch

AREA 5 Blacks and darkest shades

ebony (Fig.)	wenge	rosewood (Brazil)
African walnut	ebony stripe	goncalo alves
walnut stripe	Macassar ebony	laurel
rosewood (India)	blackbean	kingwood

AREA 6 Dark browns to darkest browns

benin	satinwood	zebrawood
teak	benge	Oriental wood
teak stripe	walnut (Fig.)	walnut (plain)
brown oak	walnut (France)	afrormosia

AREA 7 Light browns to browns

New Guinea wood	paldao	opele
elm	monkeypod	mansonia
locust	chestnut	tamo (Fig.)
persimmon	larch	narra

AREA 8 Whites to yellows and yellow tans

olive ash	white oak	prima vera
French olive ash	brown ash	peroba
sen	limba	obeche
rift oak	avodire	faux satine

AREA 9 Special effects

olive ash burl	cherry burl	imbuya burl
myrtle burl	maple burl	maidou burl
Carp. elm burl	redwood burl	madrone burl
thuya burl	kelobra crotch	white ash burl
poplar burl	vermillion stripe	gray harewood

Your color chart can be as simple as a color wheel, showing just the basic colors, or it can be elaborated to include the range of figure variations of important woods. Certainly some form of color chart showing the wide variety of woods you could be working with is a valuable aid in picture making.

Cardboard viewer. Take special care to locate the precise area of figure that expresses the object it will represent. You cannot make the perfect selection by viewing a large sheet. When following the window method recommended for knife-cutting, you automatically have a viewer to look through. You simply move the veneer square one way and another behind the window. But movement is often restricted because the window has been cut in the pattern and the pattern is fastened down to the waster wood. Overcome this limitation by tracing the window shape on a piece of cardboard. Cut the window and you now have a movable viewer to shift and turn on the chosen veneer until the perfect area is located. Cut the veneer into a manageable square and place it under the pattern window for marking. Make a movable cardboard window for saw-cutting, too. Manila file folders make good viewers.

Hard and soft sides. Veneer is not the same on both sides. When a huge knife pares a slice of veneer from a flitch, the veneer sheet flexes outward, away from the flitch, usually onto a complex of traveling belts which carry it away. Flexing compresses one side of the sheet and expands the other side, the side nearest the knife. The two surfaces retain their new characteristics. The compressed side is now known as the hard side. It feels smoother when you run your fingers over it. Pores are closer together. It takes a better finish than the open-pored, rougher side. Use the hard side for the face side of your picture unless it has a stubborn manufacturing mark or the grain is not as desirable as the soft side.

With bird's-eye maple it is especially important to make the hard side with cratered eyes the face side. The raised eyes of the soft side could pop out at some future time.

Dyeing veneers for special colors. For seascapes harewood is one of the big favorites. In America only two shades can be found. More shades are needed to depict the turbulence of a rough sea and the surge of huge breaking waves. Dyeing your own gray veneers is fairly simple.

Harewood is produced by soaking a wood which contains tannic acid in a solution of ferrous sulphate and water. The depth of gray varies with different woods, depending upon tannic content.

Ask a druggist to order a one-pound jar of ferrous sulphate of commercial grade. Or inquire at a tree nursery. Locate a good-size glass casserole dish. Avoid metal and plastic containers.

Holly produces a light gray. Birch and maple produce darker shades, depending upon the color of the wood before dyeing. Sycamore becomes quite dark and is pleasingly mottled by its natural figure. Red gumwood turns black. Oak, kelobra and butternut turn almost purple. Figured maples—curly, bird's-eye and quilted—produce highly valued figure.

The dyeing procedure is simple. Dissolve a

Harewood

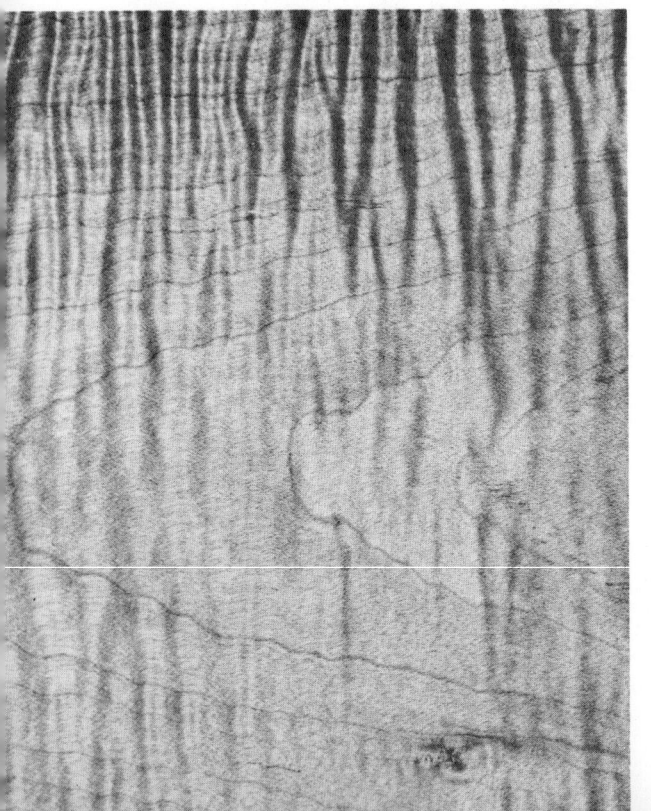

half-pound of ferrous sulphate in one gallon of water. Immerse the wood in solution. Leave it until penetration is complete; that is, until the wood is dyed through. After half an hour in solution test for penetration by cutting a sliver off an edge. If not ready the center will show original color. The color is not darkened by leaving the wood in solution for a longer time.

When penetration is complete remove veneer from the solution and wash it under a running tap. Place the veneer between sheets of absorbent paper such as brown paper bag cut to eliminate seams. Don't use newspaper. Ink will imprint the wood. Sandwich the assembly between smooth caul boards, not fir. Weight heavily or set in clamps. Change to dry paper in 24 hours and again if the wood is not dry. As a safeguard against later warp don't remove the dyed veneer from weights until you are ready to use it.

If the solution is to be stored for future use transfer it to a glass jug having a screw cap.

Home-dyed harewood has proved successful on a long-term basis. It does not stain adjoining wood; it finishes very well and holds the dyed color. However, dyeing other colors is not worth the risks. Ordinarily they come out of solution blotchy. The colors may run when being finished and they are apt to fade.

Make your own veneers. You can have fun making little pieces of unusual veneer for special eye-catching features. All around you there are shrubs, small trees, vines and prunings that might be worth slicing· into. Hopefully, some will surprise you with unusual color and figure.

The requisite for cutting such wood into thin veneer is a table saw and a good blade. Clean up the wood pieces. Remove all dirt and grit. For easy and safe handling, hand cut a piece as near to a block as possible. Set the saw fence 1/28" from the blade. Discard early cuts as necessary to provide smooth surfaces against fence and table. To get the most veneer from a block attach it to a waste block large enough for safe feeding. Two inches is about the widest slice you can produce on a home table saw.

Eucalyptus

Gumwood

Bubinga/kevazingo

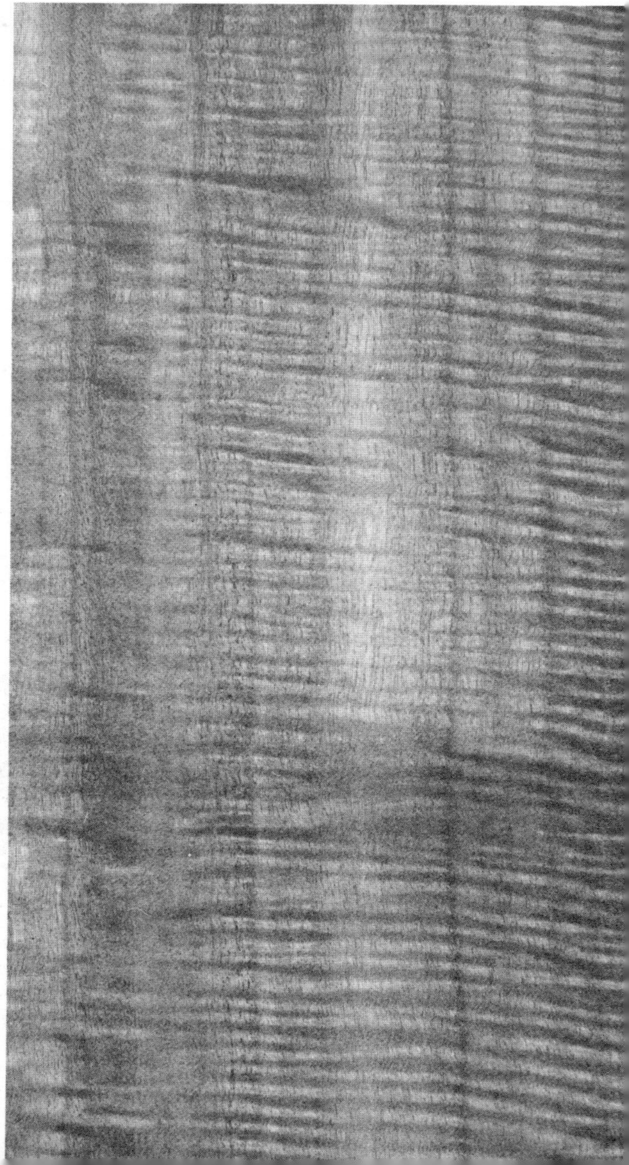

Bird's-eye maple

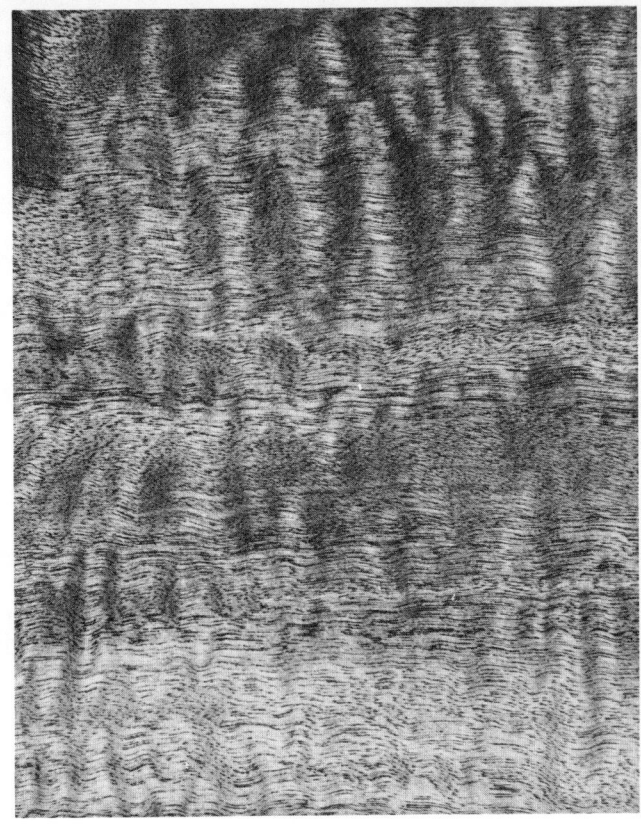

Mahogany/pommelle

Benge

Olive ash

English oak

Afara

Koa

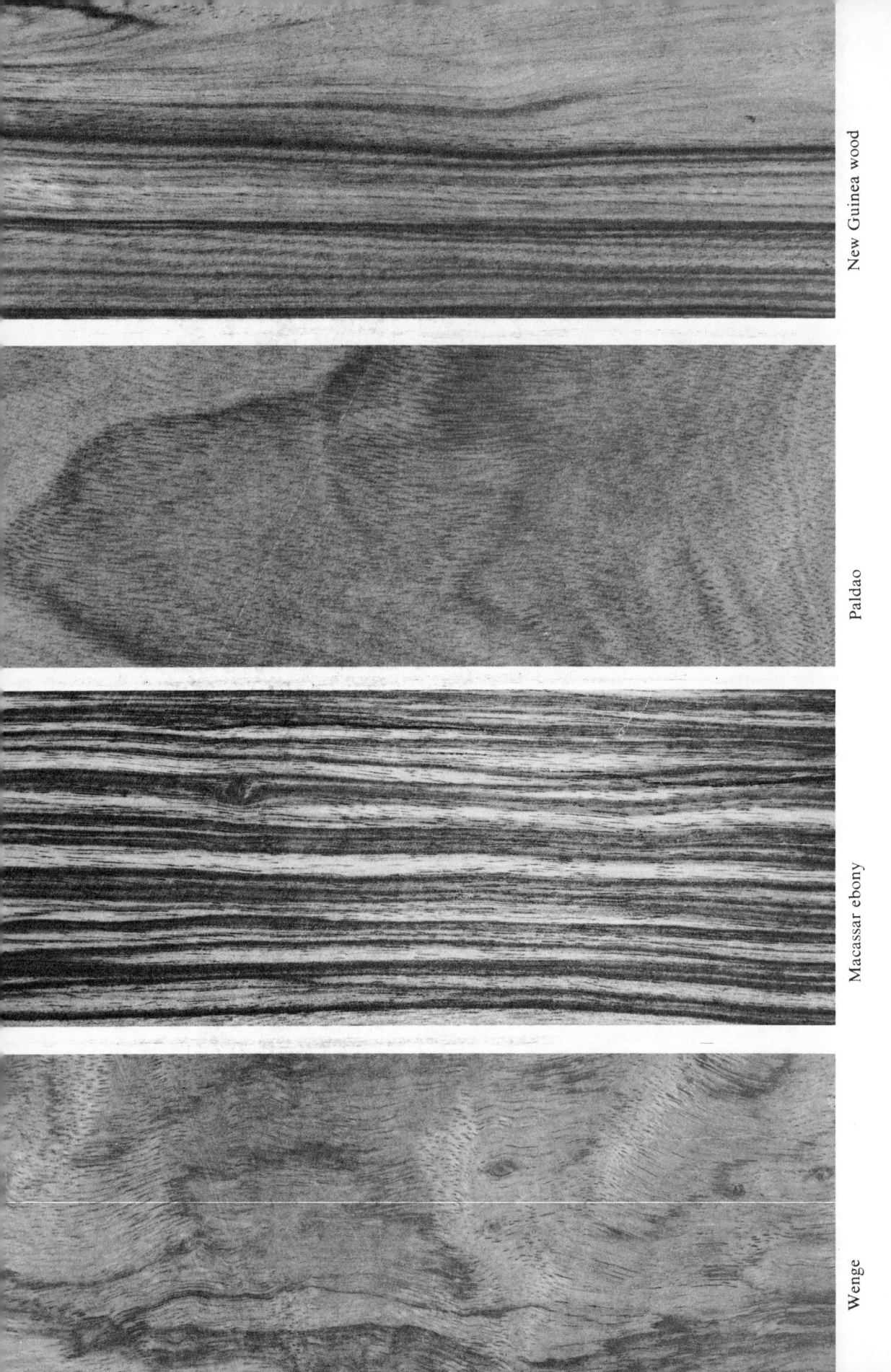

New Guinea wood

Paldao

Macassar ebony

Wenge

Brazilian rosewood

Zebrano

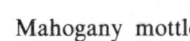

Mahogany mottle

Oak

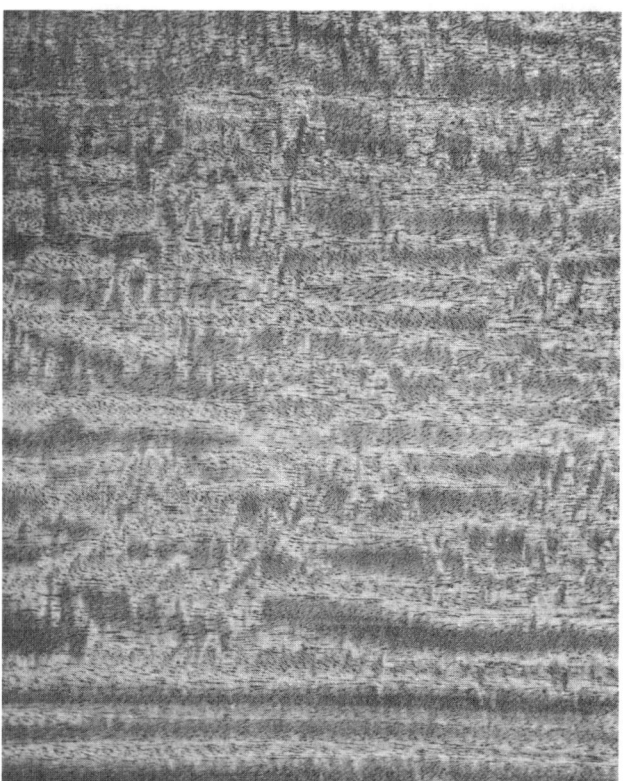

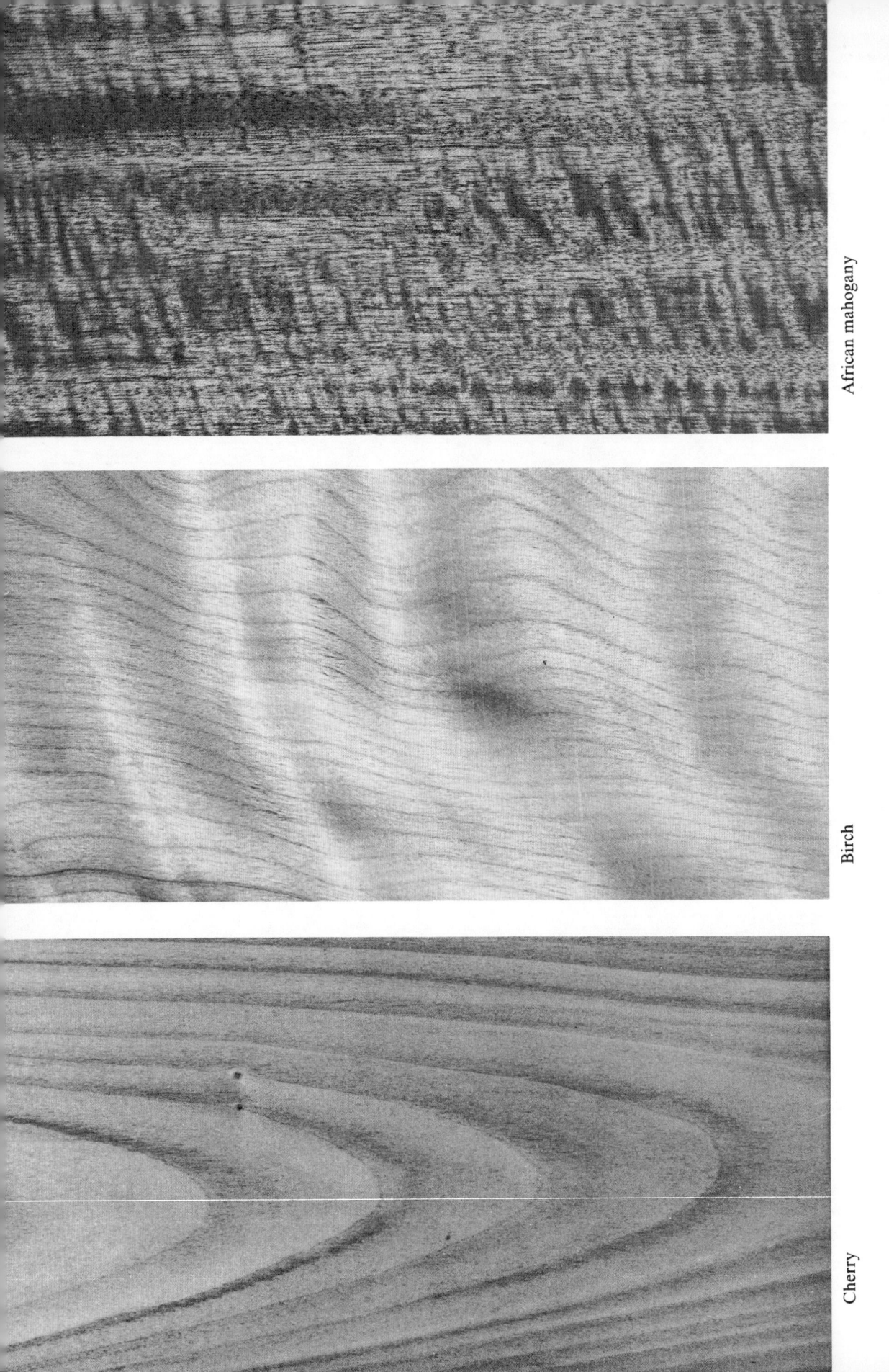

African mahogany

Birch

Cherry

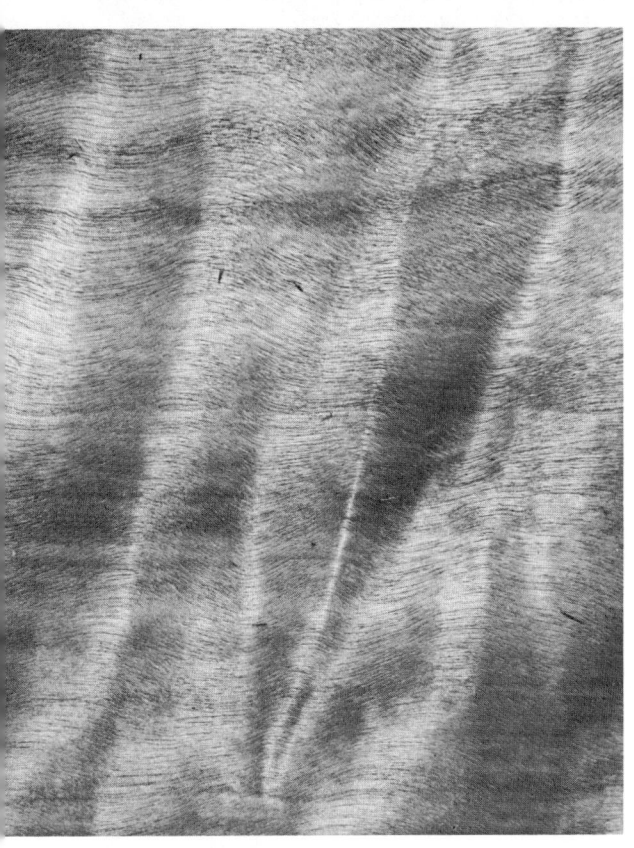

African cherry

Cedar of Lebanon

Orientalwood/Queensland walnut

Gaboon

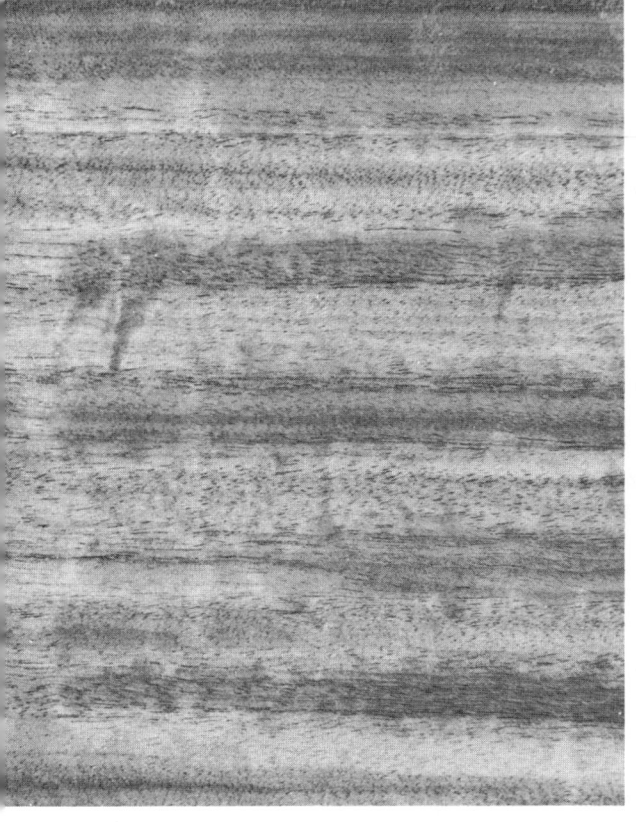

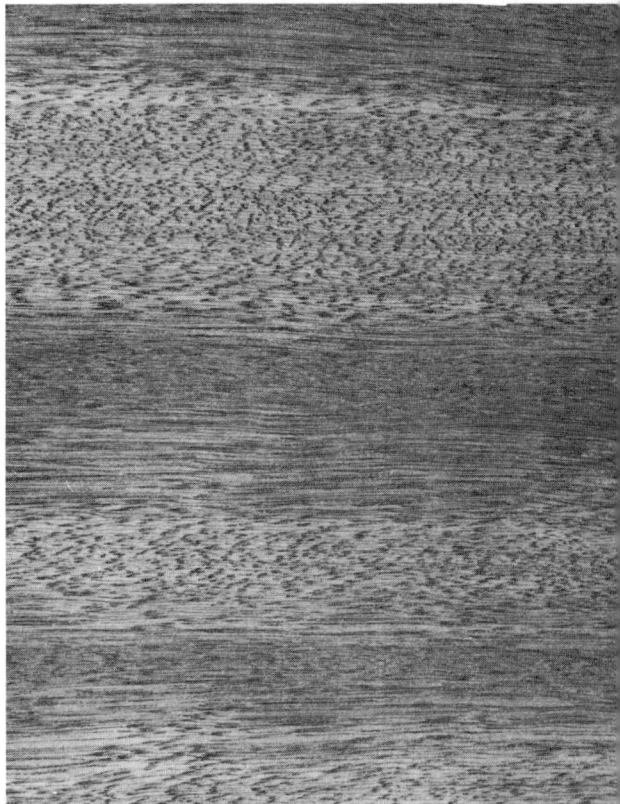

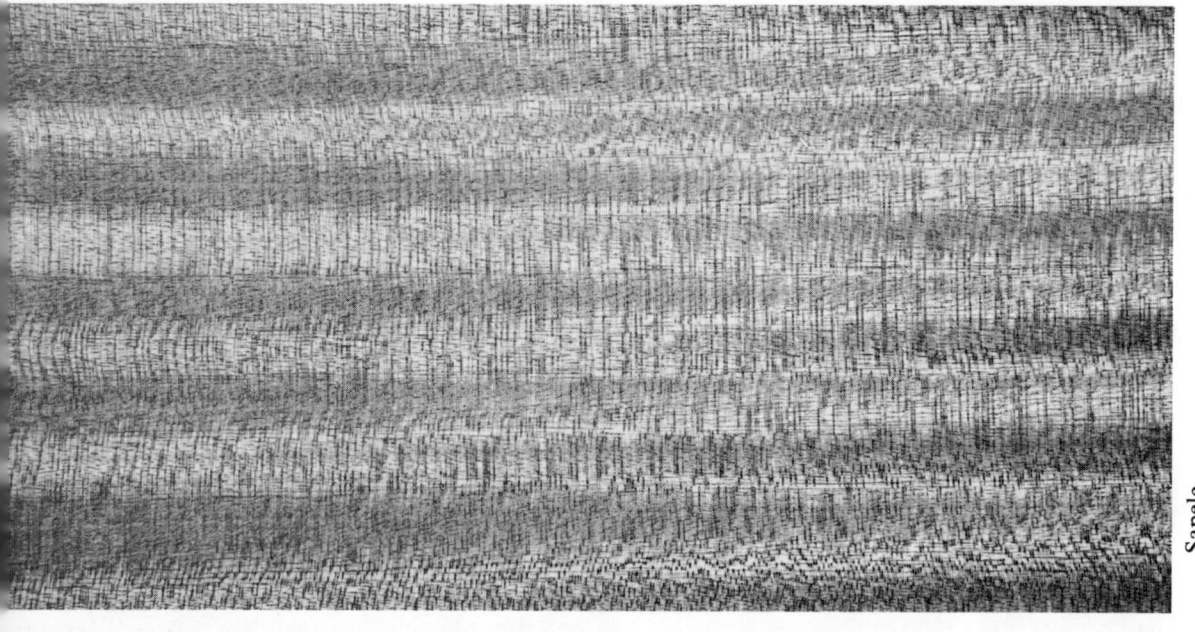

Avodire mottle

Sapele

Tola

5. Tools and equipment

There is no such thing as a Basic Workshop for marquetry. The smallest, totally functional collection of items for knife marquetry could be carried to and from the kitchen table in a shoe box. You probably could get together the things you need for less than ten dollars. However, a Convenience Workshop would contain most of the aids and tools suggested here. The listed assortment includes many items you can locate around home. You can get along without some of the items described but they are mighty convenient to have on hand. The first requirement, of course, is a sturdy table and smooth working surface.

Workboards. Particle board makes a good surface for sawing and cutting. About 18 x 18 for a start. Avoid low-test board which has too rough a surface for the purpose. You need 55-lb. test board which has a compact, smooth surface. Tempered hardboard, smooth both sides, about 12 x 12, for critical knife cutting.

Steel straightedge. Not aluminum.

Hard pencil, flat rule, scissors, tweezers, carbon paper, rubber cement.

Hand scrub brush. Smallest size. Use it to keep work surfaces clean. Prevents scratches in veneer surfaces.

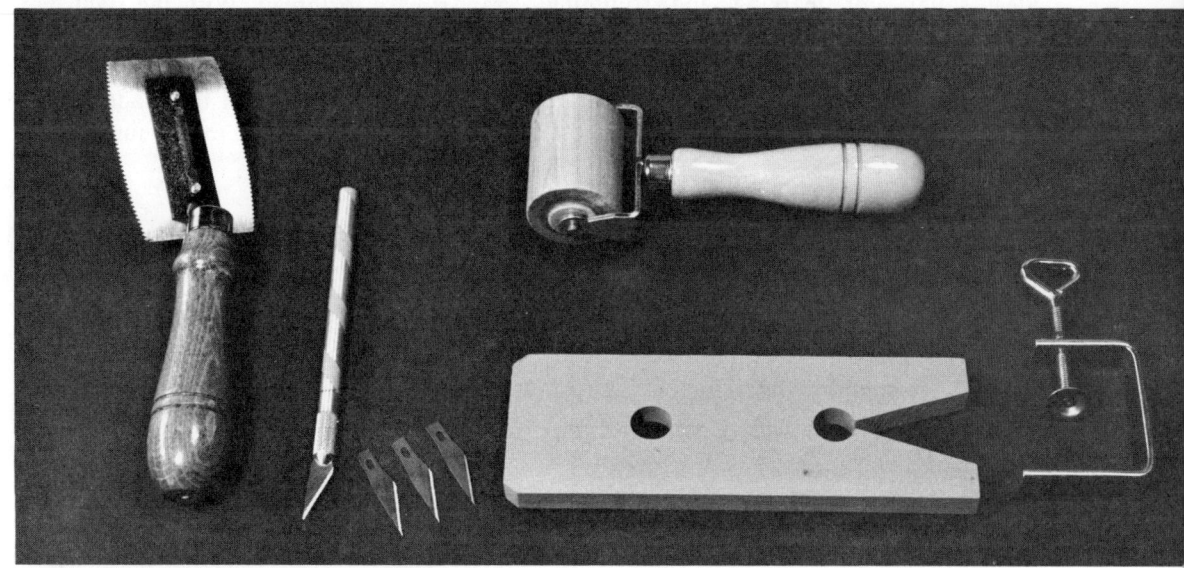

Veneer saw for cutting work-size veneer pieces. Knife for cutting marquetry designs. Bird's-mouth fret-saw table. Roller used in gluing

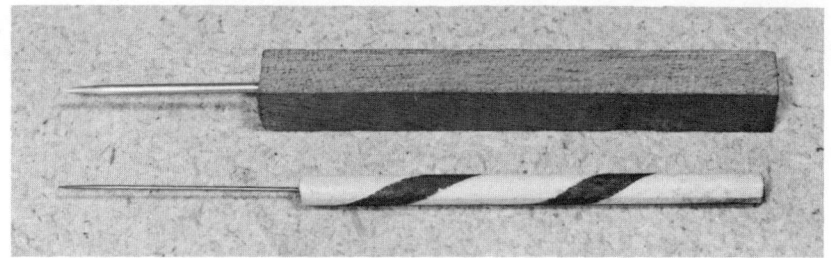

Needle with dowel handle is good device for piercing veneer to make saw-blade hole. Knitting needle segment filed lightly for scriber

Sanding block. Assorted abrasive papers.

Emery boards to improve poor joints.

Flat cardboard box lids for cut parts.

Glass jar containing a pad of Styrofoam as a visible, safe knife-keeper.

Stylus for tracing pattern lines. Choices include awl with filed point so that it will not tear pattern paper, or the head end of a large needle.

Piercing device to make a starting hole for fret-saw or scroll-saw blade. Use a pin vise, or a hat pin cut short to utilize its fancy head as a protective handle, or force a sturdy needle into one end of a 1/4" dowel 4" long.

Hard Arkansas stone for sharpening knife.

Steel square for marking and trimming veneer assemblies.

Cabinet scraper. This is a 3" x 5" piece of flat steel without a handle. It is the best tool for surfacing veneer assemblies that are ready for mounting.

Awl, point dulled with file, to keep work from slipping while spreading glue.

Wooden roller to assure tight, blister-free overall contact of glue assemblies. To be used with every type of adhesive recommended for marquetry work.

Knife. A craft knife with a slender cylindrical barrel and a knurled chuck to secure a No. 11 tapered, sharp-pointed blade. This knife is the primary cutting tool for marquetry. It costs only about one dollar. Packs of replacement blades are available. You need a knife of this type even though you plan to do most of the veneer cutting with a fret saw or power scroll saw. Other tools and equipment suggested here include optional items depending upon your chosen method. Some of the miscellany are essential items, some are just highly convenient. Many you probably already own.

Fret saw. Hand operated. Several sizes and styles are commonly used. The one to start with is the largest. It has a gooseneck metal frame that forms a 12" throat. There are two non-pivoting chucks with thumbnuts for holding a blade. The frame permits enough flexible movement to give tension to the blade. The skillful use of this saw, reducing blade breakage, requires a little practice. When you get the knack of it this large fret saw is easy to thread. With the right hand you can grip both arms of the frame and squeeze them together slightly while the left hand guides each end of the blade into the chucks and tightens the thumbnuts.

Steel square is handiest tool when trimming a veneer assembly. Knife sharpening stone. Veneer gum tape. Safety knife-keeper, cushioned

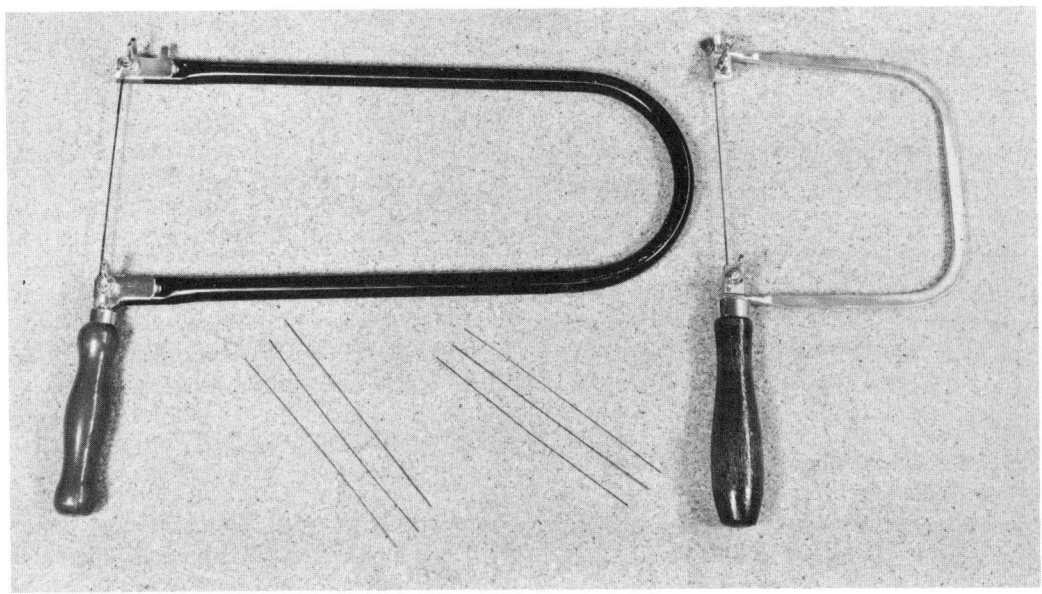

Two commercially available fret saws. Largest
having 12-inch throat is all-around favorite

Auxiliary fret saw. As a beginner you may
prefer to start with a small fret saw. Later on
when you are experienced, this auxiliary tool
will still be quite useful for sawing small
pieces. It is light in weight, well-balanced
and easier to handle than the larger, ultimate
model. The small saw to buy has a 5" throat
depth. One important feature is its swiveling
chucks. With chucks of this type you can install a blade sideways and thereby reach interior areas of work which cannot be reached
when the blade is installed normally, teeth to
the front.

Super fret saw. Many marquetarians eventually find even the 12-inch fret saw too
small for their aspirations. They end up making their own over-size homemade model.
Examples and instructions for making these
super models can be found in Chapter 18.

Bird's-mouth fret-saw table. The fret-saw
method requires a V-notched wood table
which can be clamped so as to overhang
your workbench or worktable. You can buy
a small bird's-mouth with its own special
clamp, or you can make your own. A piece
of 3/4 pine 6 x 12 or 8 x 18 with a V-notch
cut about 4" deep by 3" wide in the front

edge makes a practical table. A variation
with its own spring clamping device for holding the fret saw while you thread it is illustrated in Chapter 18. The craftsman who
uses this table made it 10 x 20.

After you have gained confidence from experience with the fret saw you may elect to
substitute your V-notched bird's-mouth for a
6-inch board with a single saw cut about
1/8" wide and 4" deep. This type minimizes
vibration of the veneer you are cutting because it provides a larger, more stable base.
It also lessens the chance of small fragments
falling on your lap or on the floor.

Blades. Fret saws take either 5" or 6" plain-
end blades. The weight of the blade for
learners is a matter of debate. Experts are apt
to recommend a medium-fine blade, but
some of us who vividly recall our early dis-
couragements from broken blades are more
apt to suggest starting with relatively heavy
fret blades having 56 teeth per inch. As skill
rises to a level of few broken blades, use a
finer blade with 64 teeth, then keep moving
up to finer blades which make smoother and
more intricate cuts. The most popular size is
No. 4/0 having 70 teeth.

Fine plain-end blades for fret saws and scroll saws are rarely found at local hardware counters. They are available from mail order suppliers. To avoid confusion between catalog listings of fret blades and jewelers blades make your selection on the basis of teeth per inch.

Blades for power scroll saws. Most operators of this power saw start with finer blades than those who use a fret saw. The power tool method involves fewer broken blades. The popular range is from No. 4/0 up to ultrafine No. 6/0.

Power scroll saw. The work of the hand fret saw can be taken over by a motorized unit called a scroll saw, formerly known as a jig saw. This is a stationary machine that is mounted with a motor on bench or stand.

Between forty and fifty years ago quite a few manufacturers were producing power jig saws. Today you cannot obtain replacement parts for those old models, but you might be lucky enough to locate a machine in good condition, long ago forsaken. If you see how to convert it to take extra-fine blades and reduce blade tension, it might be worth acquiring. First, read conversion requirements in Chapter 8.

Fortunately for marquetarians one tool manufacturer still makes a power scroll saw. The machine to buy is the Rockwell Delta 24" model. Special chucks for holding very

Type	Thickness and Width	Teeth Per Inch	Length
6/0	.008" x .016"	76	5"
5/0	.009" x .017"	73	5"
4/0	.009" x .018"	70	5"
3/0	.010" x .020"	66	5"
2/0	.010" x .021"	64	5"
1/0	.011" x .025"	64	5"
1J	.012" x .026"	56	5"
2J	.014" x .029"	48	5"
4J	.015" x .032"	40	5"
6J	.016" x .034"	32	5"
6J6	.016" x .034"	32	6"

Jewelers blades for fret saws and power scroll saws. No. 4/0 is popular size for experienced users

fine blades and special blade guides can be installed in place of standard fittings. Throat depth is 24" and cutting capacity can be extended beyond that. The table tilts to permit bevel cutting, the ultimate in marquetry techniques.

Adhesives. Most marquetarians now prefer to use a contact type of adhesive. There are several reasons for this preference. This type is known by several common names: veneer glue, contact cement and contact glue. The mutual characteristic is instant setting upon contact of two glue-spread surfaces. This feature is a great time-saver. Instead of waiting overnight before you can continue work on a mounted marquetry assembly you can handle it immediately. No clamps are needed, and this is a substantial money-saver. Another claimed advantage is that contact glue forms a better bond and is not so apt to develop blisters, but this is true only if good gluing methods are followed. Detailed gluing instructions appear in Chapter 11.

Of the various liquid glues used in marquetry the class now preferred is recognized as yellow glue for the obvious reason that its appearance is easier to remember than chemical names like aliphatic emulsion. White glue was a popular choice until yellow glue came along. Yellow glue is stronger and if properly clamped is less likely to allow blistering than white glue. Yellow is somewhat harder to spread. The applicator, either brush or wooden comb, drags a little. You have to work fairly fast to spread it uniformly on the mounting panel. It is not to be spread on the veneer assembly. Cauls and clamps are needed. White glue is now used for edge joining when cut pieces are being added to a developing picture.

Power scroll saw. The 24-in. Rockwell Delta model. Accessories needed for marquetry not on standard model, but sold separately

Rubber cement is used to apply a pattern to the waster veneer in the window method.

Glue brushes. Fiber brushes are best for contact adhesives. Nylon is somewhat easier to clean in warm water when used for applying yellow and white glues.

Cauls and clamps. Clamping equipment is essential when you use any type of adhesive except contact. Two caul boards are used to sandwich the veneer assembly and mounting panel. Particle board is preferred because of its strength, smooth surfaces and stability. It is almost warp-proof. Fir plywood is not a good substitute because the raised, irregular grain can imprint the veneer face under pressure. Particle board is easily obtained as cutoffs at most lumberyards. Half-inch thickness is heavy enough for most marquetry glue-ups.

C-clamps cost a lot less than wooden handscrews. You need at least 4 C-clamps. Six are better even on foot-square glue-ups. The best crossbearers are lengths of 1/4" x 1 1/4" an-

Best pressure system for glues requiring clamping is provided by angle irons and C-clamps

gle iron. You need two for every pair of C-clamps being used. By using angle iron crossbearers you can get by with 3" C-clamps, about half the price of 4" clamps. This equipment eliminates the need for building your own veneer press which would cost a lot more.

Homemade aids. Some very helpful devices developed by marquetarians are illustrated with instructions for making in Chapter 18.

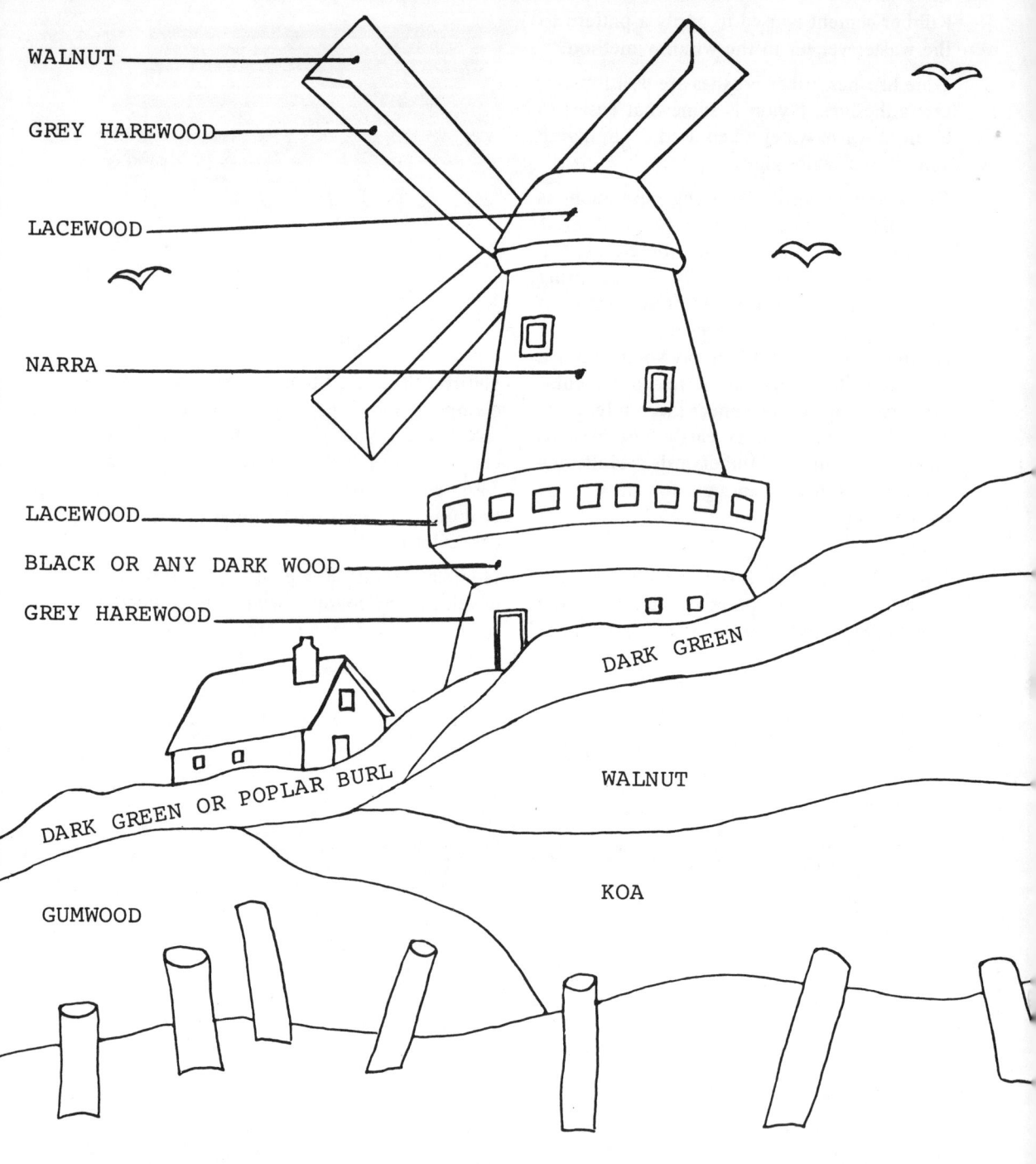

SKY - MAPLE, ASPEN OR RAMIN

WALNUT

GREY HAREWOOD

LACEWOOD

NARRA

LACEWOOD

BLACK OR ANY DARK WOOD

GREY HAREWOOD

DARK GREEN

DARK GREEN OR POPLAR BURL

WALNUT

KOA

GUMWOOD

POSTS - MAHOGANY   WATER - ZEBRAWOOD OR GREY HAREWOOD

CHANGE ANY WOOD YOU WISH, BUT TRY TO KEEP CONTRAST

6-1. "Windmill." Full-size pattern for knife-cutting window method. To make a marquetry picture of this simple subject obtain two photocopies, one as a spare. Then follow photographs step by step

48

6. Knife cutting methods — simplified and advanced

Craft knife with tapered blade is the beginner's most important tool for marquetry

The quickest way to become involved with marquetry is to buy a craft knife and a variety pack of 1/40" veneers and start cutting the elements for "Windmill." But a better way to assure permanent involvement is to get some knife-cutting practice first. Taking a little time to experiment with simple veneer shapes can quickly develop skill and confidence. Start with simple, interesting designs like tulips, turtles or tigers. By trial and mistake you soon learn how to handle the knife, how to cut veneer without breaking off the tip ends, how to avoid splitting which comes from too much pressure on the knife. Your early rewards are attractive cutouts for mounting on box top, book end, crib headboard or wall plaque.

Your next confident step as a beginner is a picture such as "Windmill" which is suitable for a marquetry first-timer. Examine the easy step-by-step procedure shown in the accompanying photographs. Start this project by getting photo copies of the full-size pattern presented here. (6-1) You already own a few of the essentials to complete this marquetry picture. The rest can be bought for a very small amount: craft knife with a pack of No. 11 blades, a sharp hard pencil, gum tape, carbon paper, sawdust filler and white glue, sandpaper, contact glue, mounting panel and clear varnish for finishing.

The picture sequence for "Windmill" was based on the window method, considered the best basic system for knife-cutting. It gets its name from the opening, or window, in the oversize sheet of waste veneer which progressively is cut away, piece by piece. One window at a time is cut. It serves as a see-through viewer and as a template for marking the cutting outline on the final veneer placed temporarily beneath the window cut in the waste veneer.

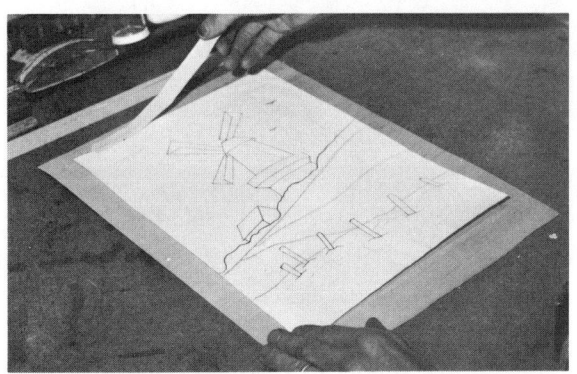

2. Select veneer for the sky. Tape pattern along top edge as hinge. Keeps pattern in register

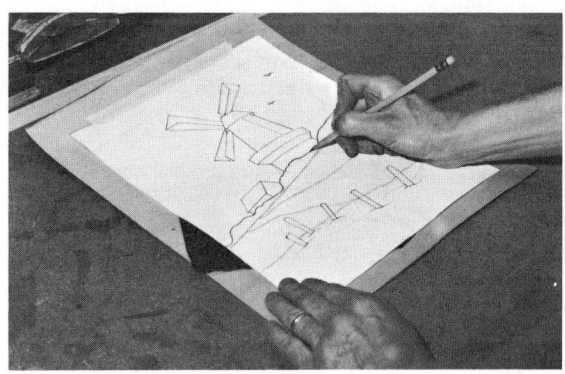

3. Place carbon under pattern. Trace line where sky meets ground. Disregard house at this time

4

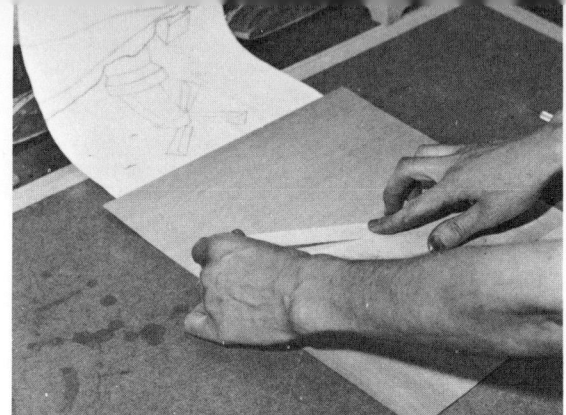

7

5

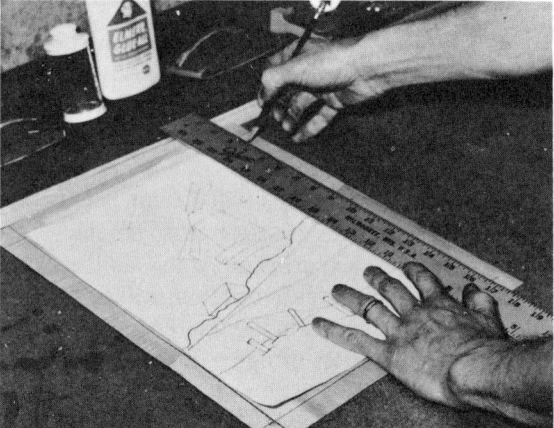

8

4. Lift pattern, cut sky/ground line with craft knife, #11 blade. Make several passes with knife

5. Lay sky veneer on piece of waste veneer. Trace cut edge of sky onto waster, using sharp pencil

6. Cut waster along pencil line

7. Fit sky and waster together. Hold in place with masking tape on back of assembly

8. Using pencil and straightedge, mark all sides of assembly as guide should pattern come loose

9. Ready to cut window for largest ground area. Trace outline for koa. Ignore posts. Cut koa to outline. Tape in place. Repeat for area marked gumwood. Trace other elements one at a time

10. At this stage, since sky is in place, windmill parts can be traced one at a time, window cut, and final veneer cut and taped in place

9

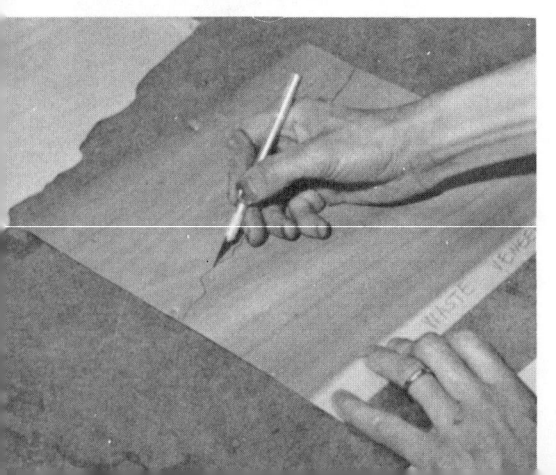

6

10

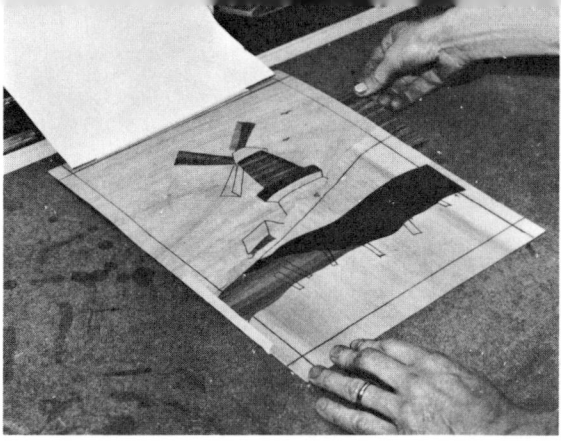

11

15

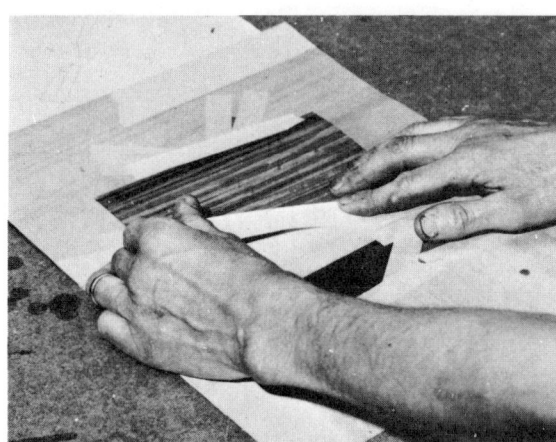

12

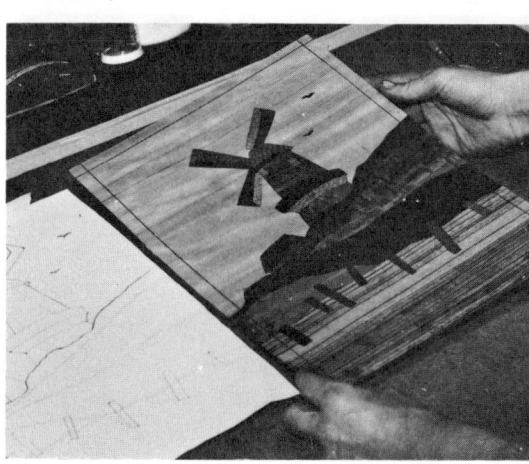

16

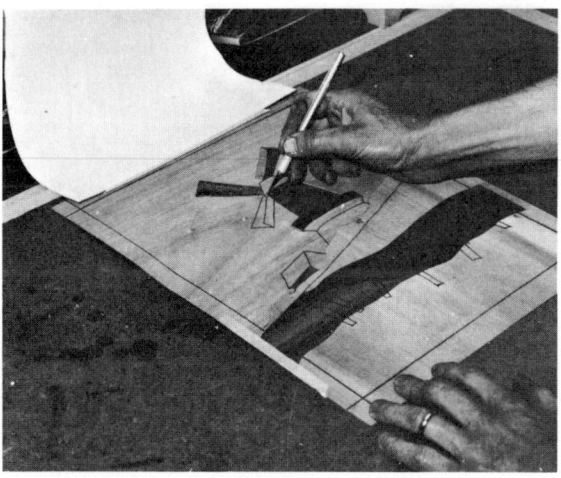

13

11. Place narra veneer under opening cut in the veneer assembly for center section of windmill. Move it until you locate best grain direction

12. Tape narra veneer temporarily on back

13. Make trackline on narra with point of knife following edge of opening in veneer assembly

14. Remove narra veneer and cut along trackline. Splintering is overcome by covering back of the veneer with gummed tape before cutting

15. Tape narra cutout into assembly. All tape on back side will be removed later. Continue until all large pieces are in place. Next, add veneer to represent water, then cut small details such as posts, windows, birds, chimney

16. Picture assembly is now complete

17. Lay tape over front to hold parts in place

14

17

18

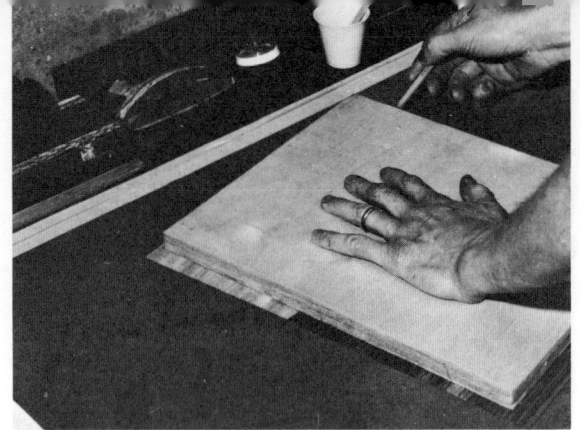

21

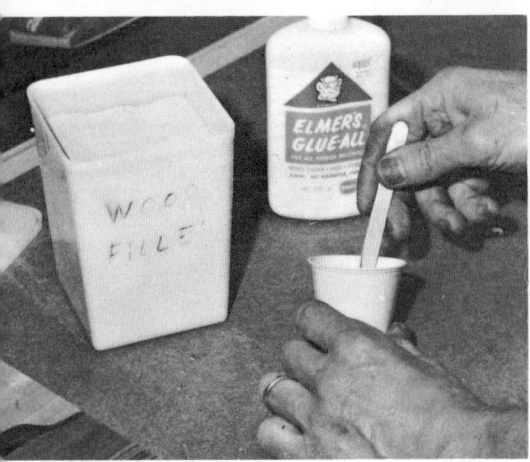

19

22

18. Remove all tape from back of assembly

19. Make up some space filler by mixing sanding dust with white glue, or buy wood filler powder

20. With putty knife, press mixture into joints in back of picture. After several hours drying time sand picture lightly to remove filler bumps

21. Cut ½" particle board mounting panel a bit smaller than veneer assembly. Center the board on top of veneer and mark around it with pencil

22. Brush contact cement on back of picture and mounting panel. Use any kind except water-base

23. After one hour, when glue is no longer tacky, nail scrap wood outside pencil lines on picture

24. Hold mounting panel over picture. Lower it flat, inside guide strips. Be certain of alignment before making contact. Press firmly

23

20

24

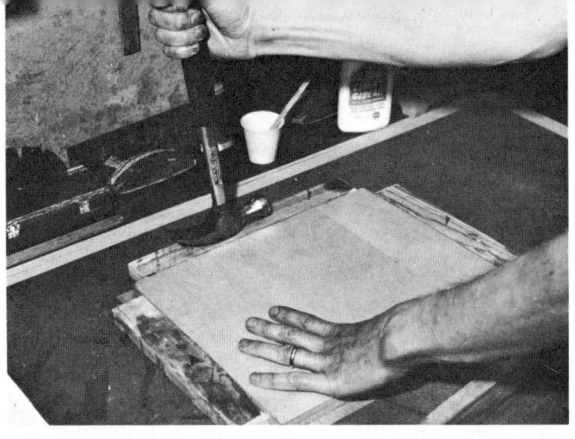

25

29

26

30

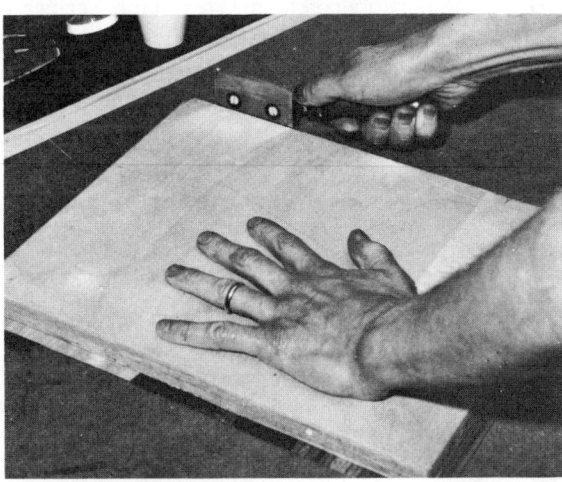

27

25. Scrap wood strips are easily removed at this time if you left nails projecting slightly

26. Roller veneer hard to assure tight overall contact and eliminate chance of blistering

27. Trim off veneer overhang. Cut around edges of mounting panel with veneer saw or craft knife. Stroke edges gently with sanding block

28. Sand face of picture. Work sanding block in direction of predominating grain. Use coarse, then medium, then fine grades of abrasive paper. Be careful not to sand through thin veneer

29. Clean off all sanding dust with vacuum brush and then wipe over surface with a tack rag

30. Apply several coats of clear varnish. Allow ample drying time. Sand lightly between coats

31. After last coat, rub with 4/0 steel wool

28

31

The next sequence uses "Swiss Lake" for demonstration. This is a more advanced method. It makes use of the window technique with the work pattern cemented to the waster instead of being hinged to the waster and used as a permanent pattern. Here, the work pattern is cut away with each section of waster. This system also goes a step closer to artistic perfection. Veneers are now cut from the back instead of the front. This procedure makes closer-fitting joints and turns out a more professional picture.

The knife point is the thinnest part of the knife blade; it makes the narrowest cut. By cutting veneer from the back, the thin knife point obviously leaves a closer joint at the front. This is the reason for the reverse cutting method. When following this system you need two reverse patterns. To make the knife-point side serve as the face of your picture you must work with a reverse pattern. In fact, you need two: one will be cut up piece by piece, the other will remain intact.

A super-sharp knife is the primary essential for cutting veneer. Buy a quality sharpening stone such as a hard Arkansas stone and use it frequently throughout every cutting session. (6-34) Apply a few drops of light household oil to the stone. Hold the knife handle and place your index finger against the side of the blade. Keep the blade at a slight angle. Press it against the stone while moving it back and forth several times. When finished cutting for the day wipe the stone clean and store in a container.

How to knife-cut veneer. Do not use heavy pressure in cutting veneers with a knife. Make several light passes with the knife over the same line until the veneer is cut through. Heavy pressure on the knife may split the veneer. Don't make little jabbing cuts, either. Move the knife slowly, steadily in the groove. Hold the craft knife as you hold a pencil. Keep the fingers of your other hand close to the knife, but never in its forward path. Do not cut from the center of a piece of veneer to the outside edge. Make all cuts from the outside toward the central mass. Cutting outward toward a tip will split it off.

Whether you purchase a kit of materials for a picture (6-35) or elect to create your own design, you need the same assortment of basic tools and materials. (6-36) Knife and blades, steel straightedge, sharpening stone, roller, rubber cement, clear tape, scriber or sharp hard pencil, veneer saw. Two reversed patterns, black carbon paper, necessary veneers and a mounting panel.

32. Apply liquid wax according to instructions on container. Pledge furniture polish preferred

33. With artist's brush, apply paint to edges of mounting panel to complete your first picture

54

Preparing patterns and waster. You have two reverse patterns, exact duplicates. Use one as a work pattern. Coat the back with rubber cement. Allow five minutes to dry. Select one piece of veneer to be used as waste, and called the "waster." The work pattern will be cemented to the waster. Be sure the waster veneer is large enough to cover the entire picture. This waster can be the veneer that you wish to use for sky, water or any large area of the picture. If you elect to use picture veneer as a waster, you save one cutting. Or it can be a sheet of uninteresting easy-cutting veneer not suitable in a picture. Even a piece of cardboard the thickness of veneers you are using can be substituted for the waster veneer.

Apply a second coat of rubber cement to the work pattern now that the first coat has dried. Lay the cement side against the waster and roller it flat.

The second reverse pattern will be regarded as the master pattern. Where you find two intersecting lines such as the upper corners of the border lines, cut two 1/4" triangular flaps. (6-37) The marks chosen for flap locations should be separated at least the full width of the picture.

You now have one pattern cemented on the waster veneer and the other having small flaps. Open the flaps and lay the master pattern over the work pattern. Carefully align the marks of both patterns. When these marks are aligned the entire patterns are in perfect alignment, or in register. You will not use the master for the first few cutting operations, but will need it as a registering device for later cutting. Preserve the register marks on the work pattern as long as you possibly can. When cutting in that area, cut away the register marks last.

Cutting procedure. Provide yourself with a smooth cutting board, never fir plywood. The panel on which you will mount the veneer picture is excellent as a cutting board. Knife scratches actually improve the glue bond. Place the waster with its work pattern on the cutting board. Before making your first cut, carefully study the pattern to determine the procedure you will follow; that

6-34. Sharpen blade often during cutting session. Hold at slight angle. Move back/forth on stone

6-35. Kit of materials for "Swiss Lake" contains variety of veneers keyed to numbers on patterns

55

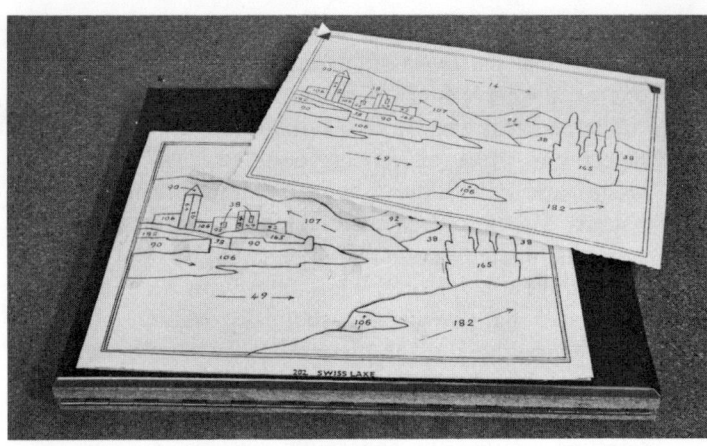

6-36. Assortment shows basic items used in knife-cutting method. Needle could replace the scriber

6-37. Duplicate reverse patterns. Flaps cut at top corners can align master over work pattern

is, the order in which you will cut the various elements.

The first element to work on should be one of the largest. The sky was chosen in the demonstration of "Swiss Lake." If your pattern design has elements which intersect other elements such as the trees intersecting sky, mountain and water, disregard the interrupters when cutting the main elements. On your waster pattern draw a continuation line for skyline right through the trees. And cut right through the trees when cutting the skyline. Later, by registering the two patterns you can trace the trees back in position on the assembled veneers.

Using your craft knife with a No. 11 blade, make your first light cut along the skyline. (6-38) You are going to cut through pattern and waster to create a window. Remember to make a series of light-pressure cuts following exactly in the path of the first cut. Many light cuts accurately made will give you an

6-38. Work pattern cemented to oversize veneer waster. First knife cut is made along skyline

excellent veneer edge and will prevent aggravation from cracked, chipped or broken edges. When you have cut completely through lift the cut piece with pattern attached out of the waster. Discard it. This entire operation of cutting out the sky is unnecessary if you have used final sky veneer as the waster. After all surrounding and inserted elements have been cut and assembled, you automatically have the sky veneer in its proper shape and position.

Now select the veneer you want for the sky. Limba was chosen for the demonstration. Place the limba beneath the open window in the waster. Move it around until the best area shows through, the most appropriate figure and texture. (6-39) Tape the limba in place on back of the waster until you can mark a cutting line around it. The window serves as a perfect template. With a hard sharp pencil, or needle or knife, trace around the window. (6-40) Remove the marked veneer and place it on your cutting board. Carefully cut along the outline. (6-41)

Remove the cut out sky and insert it into the window of the waster. (6-42) Tape it in place with transparent tape or veneer tape. When you are following the reverse method, as here, all tape should be put on the back of the veneer assembly. What we now regard as the back actually becomes the face side of the picture. Due to the wedge shape of the knife, the side nearest the cutting board will have the closest fit and that's the best side. Tape remains until the complete assembly has been glued to a mounting panel with tape side up so that it can be removed last.

Follow the same work procedure for the lake. Harewood was used here. Next, cut and insert a snow cap and then cut a piece of walnut for one section of mountain while completely ignoring the trees that will intersect that portion of mountain. (6-43)

Now that the basic elements have been cut and assembled into the waster it is time to put in the trees. Register your master pattern over the veneer assembly with carbon paper between, carbon facing the waster. Trace the clump of trees. (6-44) Set aside the master pattern. Cut out the tree area to form a window. (6-45) Slip a square of Carpathian elm burl beneath the tree window. Trace around the window to create a cutting line on the elm burl. (6-46) Move the burl to the cutting board and cut it out. Take extra care when cutting burl. It is somewhat crumbly where eyes occur at a cutting line. When cutting burls and other veneers that readily crumble or split it is good practice to cover the back completely with veneer tape. Tape will hold the veneer intact while you handle and cut it.

Insert the tree into the waster. (6-47) Next, cut a complete plateau in the foreground, ignoring the setback. When in place cut a window for the setback piece. Continue in this way, inserting mountain and distant shore before attempting any part of the chalet. Notice that the completed veneer assembly is still framed by the waster. (6-48)

Use a steel square or steel straightedge to square up the picture. Cut off the waster frame and excess veneer.

Marquetry pictures are seldom framed with molding. Veneer borders, stringers and inlay strips are frequently applied. Instructions for bordering, filling and finishing appear in later chapters.

The demonstration for "Swiss Lake" was based on an enlarged pattern made from the smaller pattern in a standard kit for a 5 x 7 picture. The picture was completed with all detail contained in the pattern. However, depending upon your level of skill, you could have stopped somewhere along the way, omitting delicate detail. At any of several stages, you would have turned out a beautiful picture. (6-49)

Reverse bevel cutting from front

Most instruction books in advanced marquetry advocate knife-cutting from the back of veneer to leave the plowed-up lip on the glue side. This practice makes the tightest joints on the face.

The following innovation allows front-cutting without leaving a wide joint. If nothing else it gives the artist-in-wood the option of working from either side as preferred. Front-cutting is especially useful for very hard woods, such as rosewood, ebony, laurel, which are difficult to cut cleanly and which

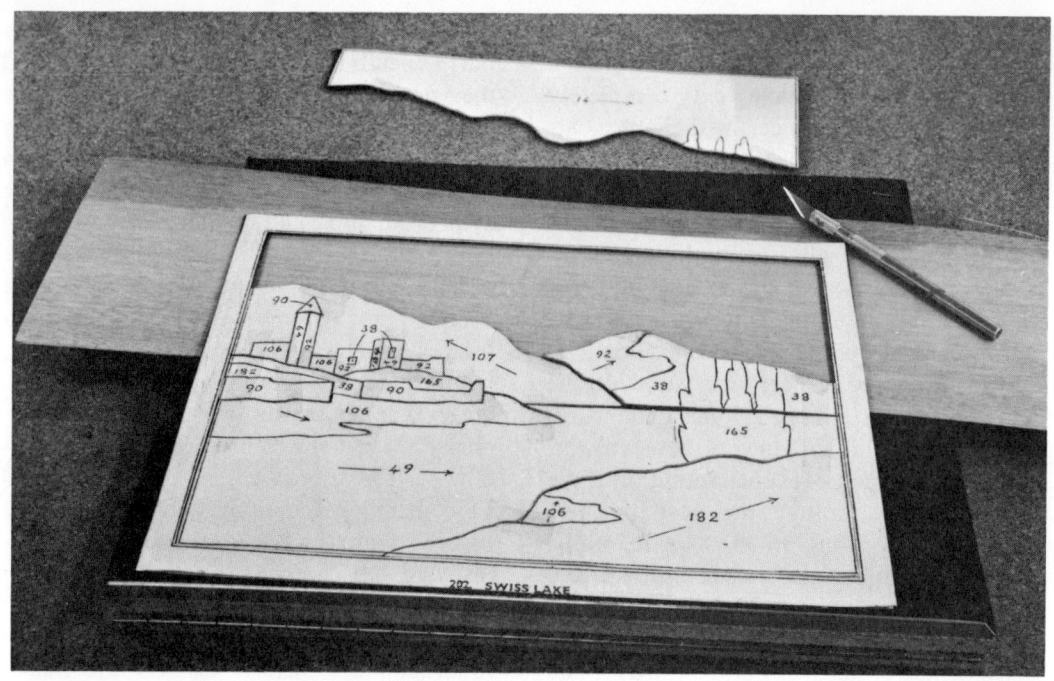

6-39. Sky waster and pattern removed to create
window for viewing limba veneer to become sky

6-40. Window serves as template for pencil to
trace sky outline on selected area of limba

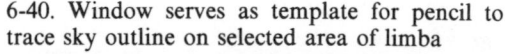

6-41. Knife makes first light cut along pencil outline of sky. Veneer is on smooth workboard

6-42. Sky piece is inserted into waster and is held in position with tape applied on the back

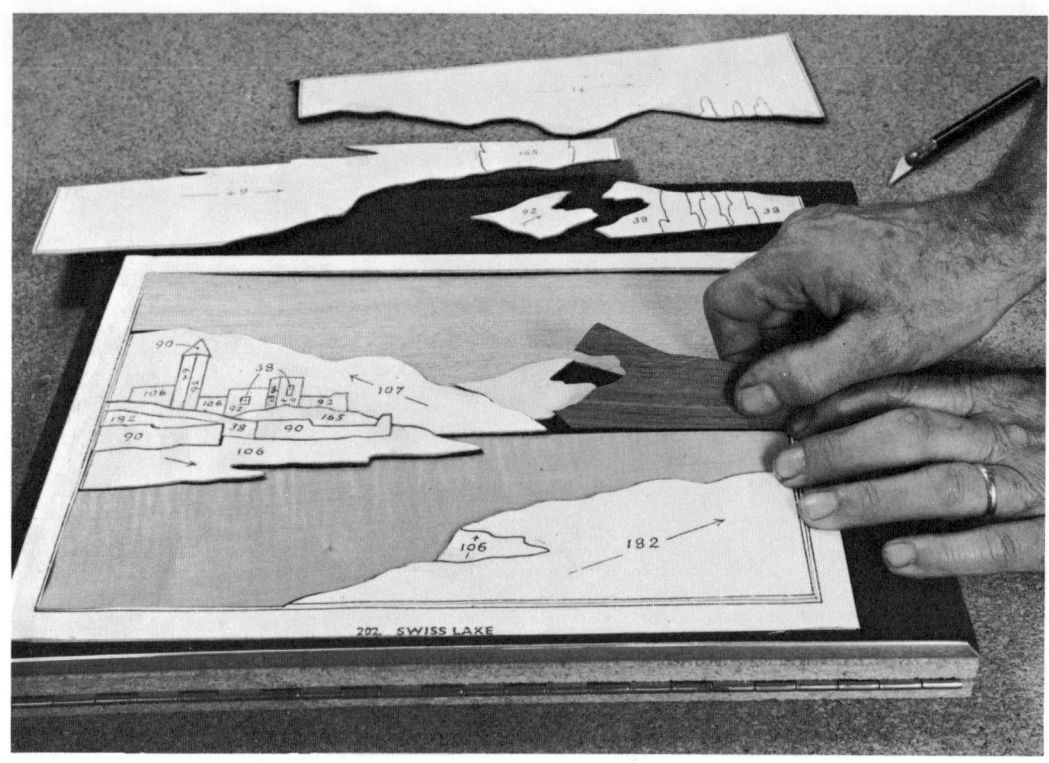

6-43. Harewood lake and snow cap have been cut
and inserted. Walnut mountain ignores the trees

6-44. Master pattern registered over waster so
trees can be traced on lake, mountain and sky

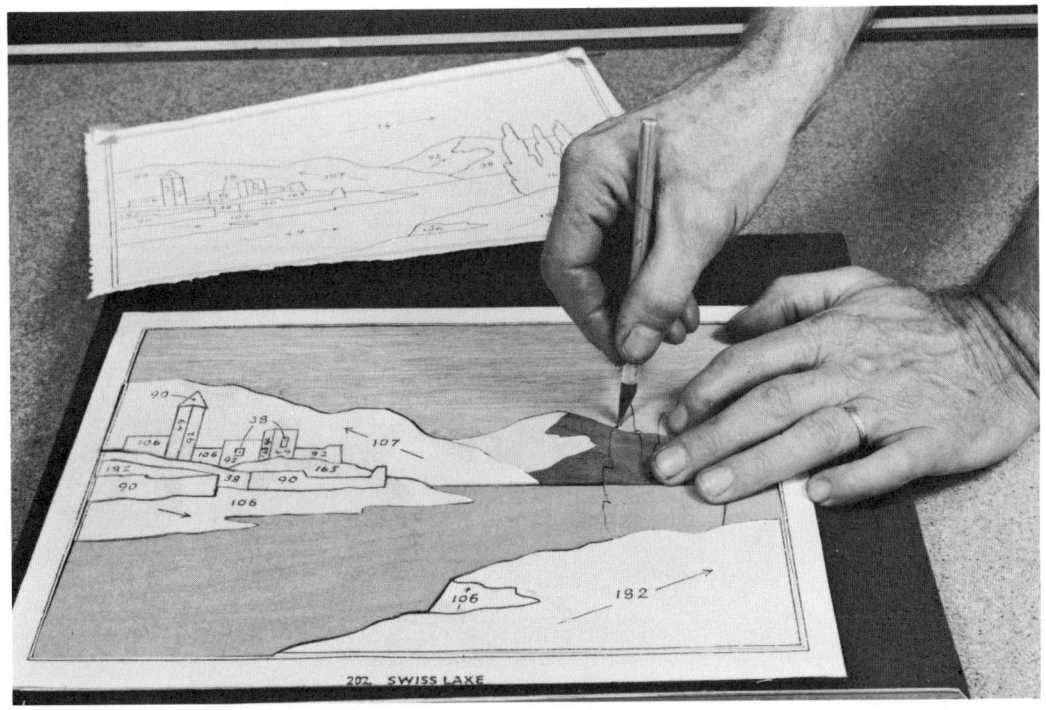

6-45. With master pattern removed, tree window
in veneer assembly is now accurately cut out

6-46. Tree window is perfect template for marking
cutting outline on elm burl under window

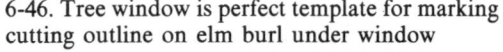

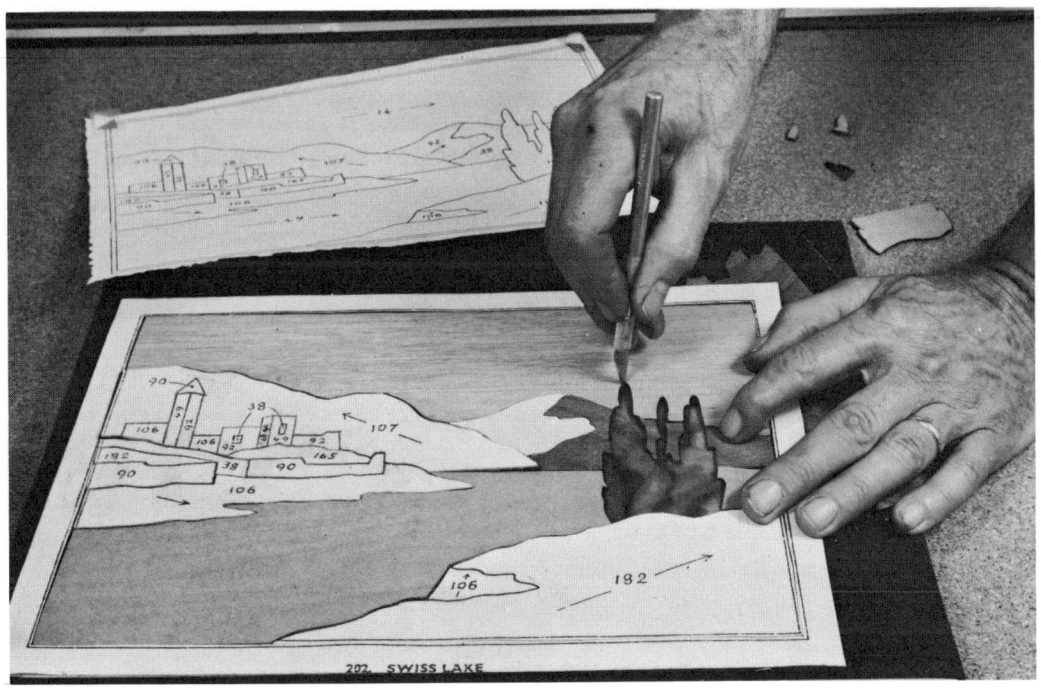

6-47. Tree clump cut from elm burl is inserted into veneer assembly and taped on reverse side

6-48. Mountains, far shoreline, plateau; then setback and chalet. Completed reverse assembly

may feather on the bottom edge. With front-cutting these defects will be on the glue side and will not show in the picture. (6-50)

The first cut is made through the main veneer on the pattern line at a bevel angle of 15 to 20 degrees to create a window. The smaller bevel angle is best for thick veneers.

Tape the inlay veneer beneath the main veneer window. Knife-score the inlay veneer at the same bevel used to cut the window. Cut only deep enough to leave a cutting line for the next step. Do not cut deeply. You can visually judge the angle and the mating bevel cuts involved in this method.

Remove tape and separate the two veneers. Now complete the cutout for the inlay veneer. Follow the scored line, but this time with the bevel reversed. The bevel angle should be the same as used in previous cuts.

Position the inlay in the window of the main veneer. Overlap should be no more than .010 to .015, the ideal being about .005. (Playing cards are about .011.) Large windows and inlays tolerate a larger overlap. If satisfied with the fit remove inlay, coat edges with white glue, replace. Invert the assembly onto wax paper laid on a smooth worktable.

6-49. Four stages, starting upper left, at which picture could have been considered complete

Roller the main veneer down over the inlay, working uniformly around the window. Rollering causes the lipped edges of the bevels to crush together to form a tight seam. Glue softens the veneers and lessens the stress. When the face surface is flush clamp for 30 minutes. Remove clamps, peel off wax paper and leave uncovered for 10 minutes to stabilize moisture content and to relieve stresses from the harsh pressure. Apparent irregularities along the joint will disappear in sanding.

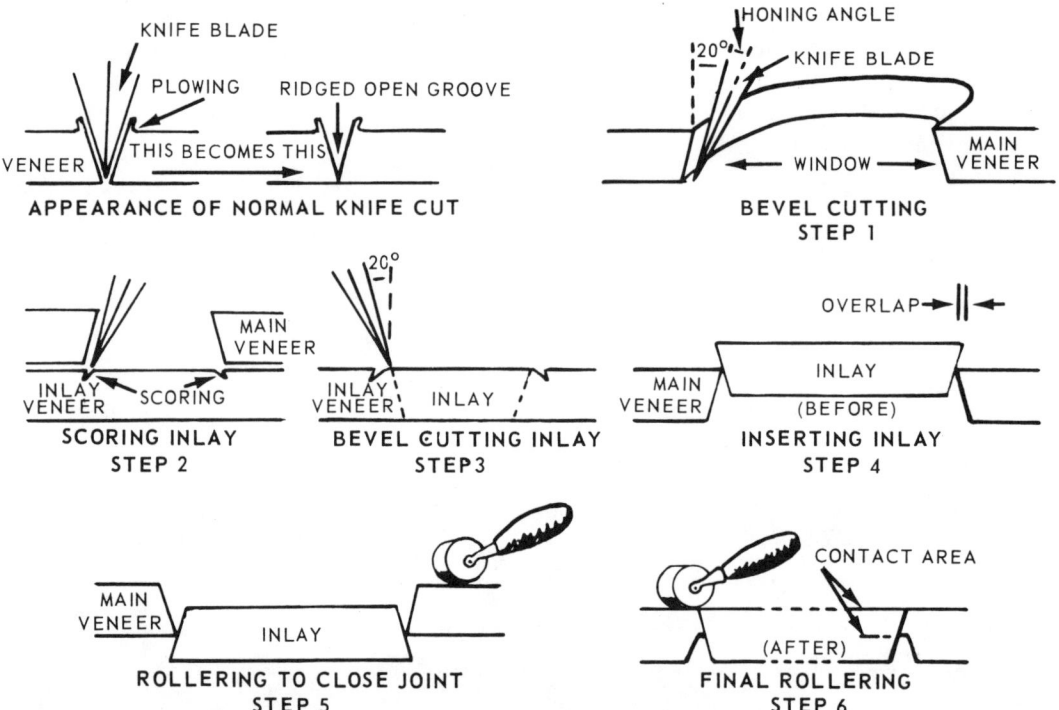

6-50. When front-cutting is considered desirable for some elements of a picture the reverse bevel method can be combined with the advanced system of cutting from the back for the tightest joints

7. Techniques of fret-saw cutting

The hand-operated fret saw is regarded with considerable respect by many marquetarians. It is virtually a one-tool marquetry workshop and a low cost one at that. The fret saw is capable of cutting the most intricate designs with ease and precision. Veneers that are difficult to cut with a craft knife can be cut cleanly and accurately with the fret saw. The knife, however, is not permanently retired when you own a fret saw. Many marquetarians use both tools to complete a picture. The fret saw may be substituted for the knife in the window method illustrated in the making of the "Windmill" picture, Chapter 6. The fret saw also is used with the pad method of making pictures, Chapter 9.

In this chapter two marquetry methods are described. First, in the practice session, each element is cut individually and taped to neighboring elements piece by piece. In the second method the waster and veneer to be inserted into the waster are cut simultaneously at an angle so that the closest possible joint is made in a single saw cut.

Two styles of commercial fret saws are shown in Chapter 5. If you intend to have only one, the most useful has a 12-inch throat. Instructions for making your own extra-large saw when you are ready for it can

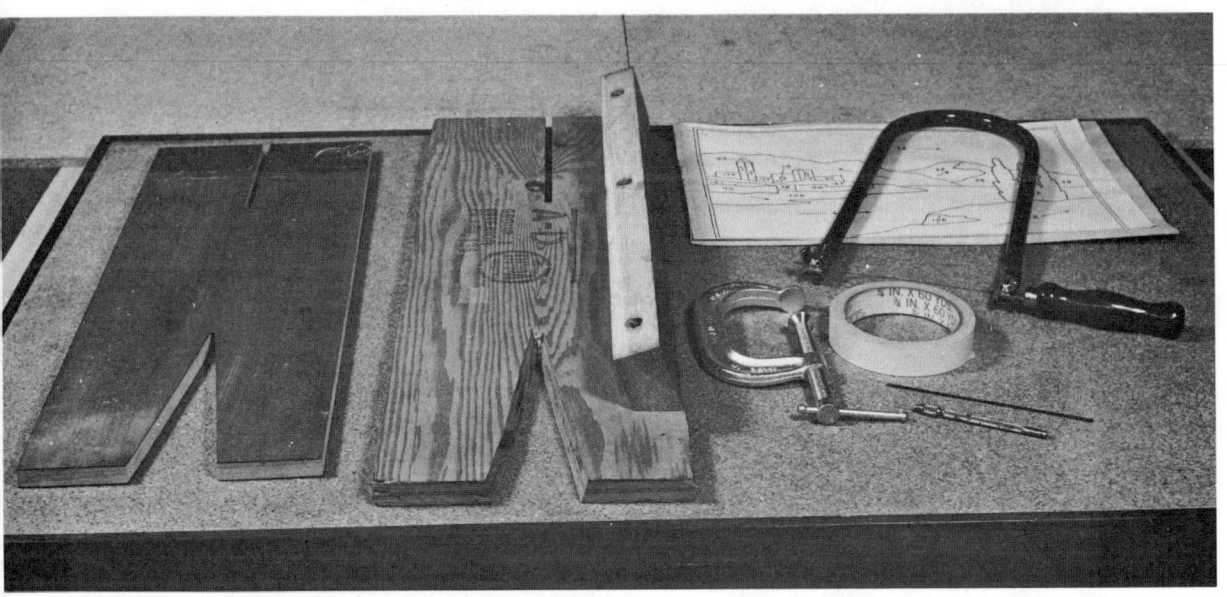

7-1. Bird's-mouth saw tables. Left, for cutting flat. Second style has beveled cleat to provide a sloping table for angle-cutting method

be found in Chapter 18. All fret saws used in marquetry must have chucks that are able to take plain-end blades.

Fine jewelers piercing saw blades used by experienced marquetarians range from 1/0 coarse with 64 teeth per inch to 6/0 fine with 76 teeth per inch. The most popular size is 4/0 with 70 teeth. It readily cuts veneer and other marquetry material such as metal, ivory and bone.

A single sheet of veneer is too fragile to be cut to shape with a fret saw without a suitable support or table underneath. Veneer must be supported beneath the point where the blade is operating. This is accomplished by a simple device called a bird's-mouth, usually a piece of 3/4 plywood or pine with a V-notch cut in one end. (7-1). The other end is clamped to a worktable or bench so that the notch extends beyond the worktable.

After you have selected your fret saw and blades it is advisable to practice placing the blades in the clamps of the saw. When you have placed the blade in the saw clamps under tension try cutting a few scraps of veneer. Too little tension will allow the blade to follow the grain of the veneer, and too much tension will cause excessive blade breakage. A few practice cuts will enable you to determine what the proper tension is for you and your saw.

When you have determined the proper tension for your saw by making several practice cuts in scraps of flat veneer take the next practice step. In another scrap of veneer use a pin or needle to pierce a hole in the veneer about 1/2" from the edge. Thread a blade through this hole, teeth pointing down and away from the throat. Clamp the blade in the saw clamps under proper tension and make several practice cuts. At this point, when threading the blade, you will wish you had

7-2. Small pieces of flat veneer can be sawed without scrap veneer reinforcement beneath

two more hands; however, threading becomes easier with practice. A blade threading fixture is illustrated in Chapter 18.

Often the veneer can be cut on the saw table without additional reinforcement. Enough support is provided by the bird's-mouth when sawing is done near the vertex of the V-notch. (7-2) Should the veneer seem especially brittle, soft or crumbly, or even if strong grain closely parallels a portion of outline, you will want to play safe by taping a waste scrap piece of veneer beneath the area of veneer which has the outline on it. (7-3) Many selected pieces are one of a kind, too precious to ruin by splitting.

Sometime you will want to cut a piece of veneer that is slightly warped. Taping it to a single thickness of scrap veneer underneath may not straighten out the warp. In this case if no suitable substitute is on hand you may have to resort to the pad method. Sandwich the warped piece between two pieces of 1/28 poplar or other soft, stable wood. (7-4) Arrange the grain of each sheet of veneer in the pad so that no two adjoining sheets have parallel grain. Apply masking tape tightly at several points around the pad. Cement the pattern outline on the top poplar blind. Pierce the pad for the saw blade and cut the entire assembly. Because the piece was flat when being sawed it will fit into the picture and flatten permanently when glued to a mounting panel.

If you must use a badly warped piece, or even a large piece that is only slightly warped, flatten it by moistening both sides. (7-5) Lay it between wrapping paper. Place particle board top and bottom. Set heavy weights on top. Leave the assembly for at least 12 hours. Repeat if necessary, using dry paper. Don't cut until it is dry.

7-3. Half-pad method of using piece of scrap veneer underneath is safer way for beginner

7-4. Pad method of sandwiching warped veneer keeps it flat and protected while being sawed

7-5. Badly warped veneer is easily flattened by moistening and weighting for one or two days

Practice session. Consider your first experience with the fret saw as a trial run, not intended to produce a masterpiece. Select a simple pattern with little detail. If the scene has small elements ignore them. As an example of an appropriate first pattern we have further simplified the "Windmill" design presented for beginners in knife-cutting, Chapter 6. Our simplified version (7-6) is too small to work with. Go back to the full-size pattern. Make two copies on tracing paper, but omit details that are not included in the small version here. Besides the duplicate patterns and a starter assortment of veneer the main items needed are a flat bird's-mouth saw table clamped so the V-notch extends beyond your worktable, a fret saw and plain-end blades. Many experts use nothing coarser than a 4/0 jewelers blade having 70 teeth per inch. However, you are likely to get more encouragement from your practice session if you use a stronger blade having only 56 teeth per inch. You will break fewer of these blades.

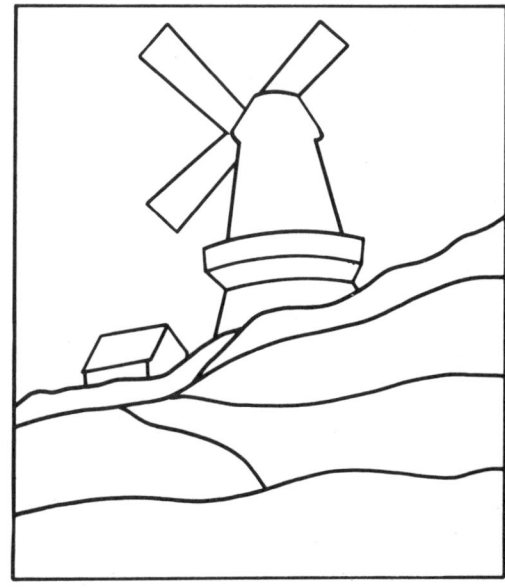

7-6. This version of "Windmill" shows how you can simplify a scene and retain the story idea

This practice session uses a simplified pattern of "Windmill." Each element is traced on chosen veneer, cut out as an individual piece and then assembled piece by piece on a duplicate pattern

7-7. Simplified version of "Windmill" was made
as a beginner's fret-saw practice project

Tape one of your simplified patterns to a
smooth workboard. Then lay the second pattern on top of the piece of veneer you have
chosen for one large element. Trace the pattern for that element with the head of a
sturdy needle or similar stylus. A stylus
avoids heavy pencil lines on the pattern. A
fine pattern line must be retained for tracing
an accurate line on the joining piece.

In this beginners' exercise you should start

with the half-pad (7-3) system of reinforcement. Tape a waste scrap of veneer directly
under the traced outline of your selected
veneer. Pierce the assembly for a blade. Insert the jewelers blade about halfway
through the veneer. Teeth must point down
and away from you. Lay the assembly on the
saw table with the blade over the V-notch,
half above, half below. Move the fret saw
into sawing position with lower chuck and

handle directly below the projecting saw blade. Attach the blade to the lower chuck. Hold the saw frame motionless or you will snap your first blade. Next, maneuver the upper chuck into engaging position with the upper end of the blade. With your right hand squeeze the saw frame very slightly. Tighten the chuck with your left hand. You are ready to go. Saw frames differ but all require compression to establish light tension on the blade. Threading the saw with a delicate blade becomes somewhat easier with practice, as you will very soon discover.

The sawing operation. Hold the fret saw in a perfectly vertical position at all times. Pump the frame in about a 2-inch travel up and down. Cutting is done on the down stroke. Keep the frame in a fixed position; that is, don't swing it. *Move the veneer into the path of the saw blade.* Keep the blade safely within the V-notch as far forward toward the vertex as reasonably possible, where the veneer has the most support underneath. Hold down the veneer with your fingers close to the blade. Give special attention on the up-travel when the saw is apt to lift the veneer. When making a sharp turn or cutting a point, move the veneer slower but keep the saw moving up and down. Forcing veneer too fast into the path of the blade will break the blade. Where a picture element such as a building requires an interior opening for door or window, pierce a new starting hole. Use a sturdy needle stuck in a dowel handle or use a pin vise.

After cutting each piece lay it on the pattern that you taped to your worktable. Join the piece to its neighbor with masking tape or gum tape. Clear tape is not wholly dependable on the face of picture elements for the reason that it may leave a gummy residue or it may even pick up a fragment of veneer, especially near the cut edge of soft veneer. Gum veneer tape requires a small amount of moistening for removal, but consequent warp can be avoided if you keep every veneer assembly under weights when not working on it.

Your excitement will grow as the picture continues to develop with the addition of each new piece. (7-7) Be patient. Don't be easily satisfied with an element that doesn't fit well. Make it over. With practice your cutting skill with the fret saw will develop rapidly. And fewer blades will break as you learn the tricks of handling the versatile fret saw. It's an amazingly capable tool!

If you prefer to undertake "Swiss Lake" instead of "Windmill" for practice, this subject, too, can be simplified. Toward the end of Chapter 6 four versions each increasing in complexity are shown. (6-49)

Simultaneous Bevel Cutting

The next method is the one followed by the more advanced marquetarians. The technique involved is intended to produce a better picture. Improvement shows up in closer-fitting joints between various elements of a veneer composition. There are two variations from the previous system. All cutting is done at an angle, called the bevel-cutting method. And cutting of waster and insert pieces is done in one pass of the saw, called simultaneous cutting. This is the method to learn when you feel satisfied with work you have accomplished with simpler techniques. The picture subject for this demonstration will be "Swiss Lake" so that the new techniques may be compared closely with techniques applied earlier to the same picture.

Equipment. Two patterns, carbon paper, fret saw and blades, clamp, sharp needle, bird's-mouth saw table, roller, rubber cement, white glue, Magic transparent tape or veneer tape, knife and steel straightedge.

Start by coating the back of one pattern with rubber cement. Allow about five minutes to dry. Select one piece of veneer to be used as waste. This piece will be called the "waster." Your work pattern will be cemented to this waster. The waster can be waste veneer or the veneer you select for the sky, water or any large area of your picture. Be sure the waster is a little larger than the entire pattern.

Apply a second coat of rubber cement to the work pattern which already has been coated once. Place this pattern on the waster (7-8) and roller it flat.

Take your second pattern, to be called the

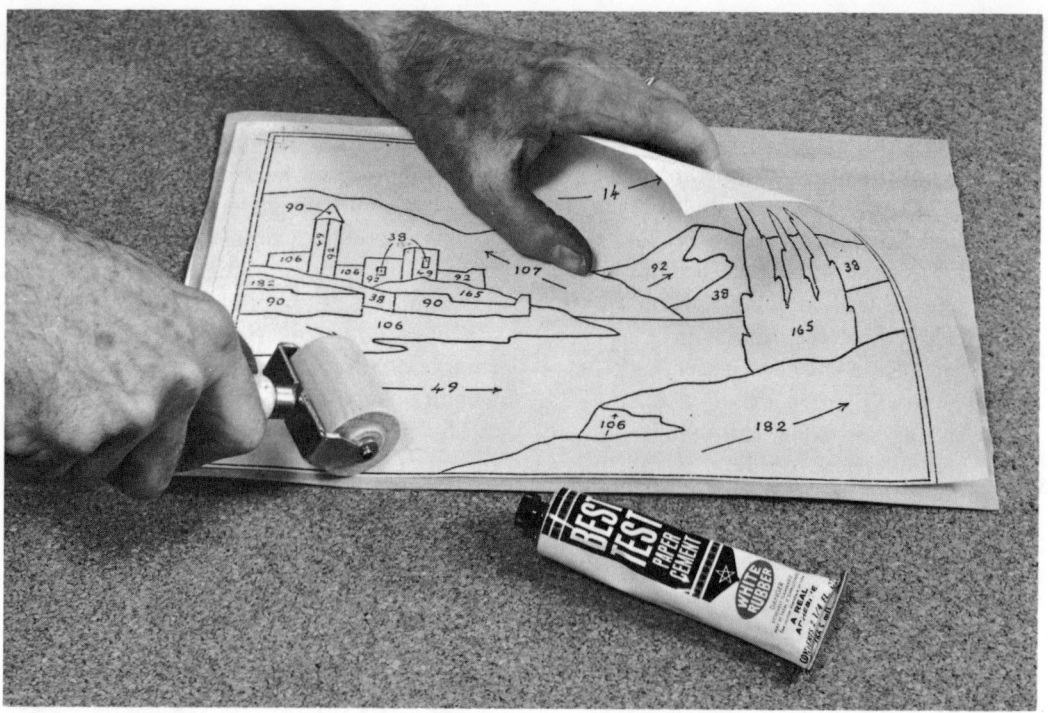

7-8. Work pattern, exact duplicate of master, is cemented to oversize veneer sheet called waster

"master," and cut two 1/4" triangular flaps over any two markings. The corner where borders intersect are ideal. (6-37) The distance between these two marks should be at least the width of the picture.

You now have the work pattern cemented to the waster and the master pattern with small flaps cut through. Open the flaps and lay the master pattern over the work pattern. Carefully align the marks of both patterns. When these are lined up the two patterns will be perfectly aligned, or in register. When you are cutting veneers leave the register marks as long as possible. By preserving the marks you can always align one pattern to the other. Set aside the master pattern to an area of your work space where you can see it. You will not use it until some basic cutting has been done.

If you have made a bevel-cutting bird's-mouth (7-9) clamp it to your table with the entire mouth of the V-notch overhanging. If you have only the flat style of bird's-mouth place a wedge beneath it on the left side to

raise the saw table to an angle of about 12 degrees. Work with the same wedge all of the time so that the angle, whether exactly 12 degrees or a bit off, will remain constant for all of your work.

Bevel Cutting. For a perfect joint the following work rule must be observed. When the left side of the bird's-mouth is raised move the veneer in a clockwise rotation into the saw. If the right side of the bird's-mouth is raised move veneer in a counterclockwise rotation. By holding your saw constantly vertical, by having the saw table raised to the proper angle and kept at the same angle for

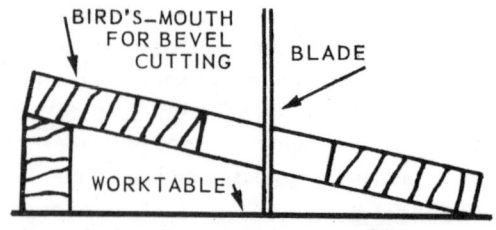

7-9. Cross section shows V-notched bird's-mouth with block raising left side for bevel cutting

all work, and by adhering to the proper direction of rotation, you compensate for the thickness of the saw blade. With clockwise rotation the left side of your bird's-mouth must be raised 12 degrees, then the portion of the top veneer upon which the pattern is cemented will be undercut, while the bottom veneer—the selected piece—will be short-beveled on its top surface. When the two pieces are assembled they telescope together to form a perfectly tight fit that requires little or no filler.

Cross section drawings (7-10) show the rather complicated relationship between the tilted saw table and the direction of feeding work into the saw blade. Notice that changing the direction of feed (A) and (B) changes the assembly method for the insert, and that changing the table tilt (7-11) from left to right (C) and (D) also changes the assembly method. These principles apply only to fret-saw work in which the blade always cuts away from you. In power scroll-saw work the blade cuts toward you and this factor reverses the rules for bevel cutting. These apparent complications will evaporate the next time you settle down in front of either cutting tool and have the accompanying draw-ings, or those in Chapter 8, to guide you.

A good element to make first is the largest in the scene, the sky. The best place to start on "Swiss Lake" is the line between sky and mountains. After selecting the area to be cut, choose the veneer for this area and tape it (7-12) to the back of the waster. Avodire was chosen for the sky in this demonstration. Be sure the selected veneer is positioned to give you the desired portion.

Using your needle or pin vise (7-13) pierce a hole through the two pieces of veneer at the same time. Select a point where two lines of the pattern intersect to make this pin hole. Lay this veneer pad assembly, pattern up, on the saw table. Install the blade with the teeth of the blade pointing down and away from the throat of the saw frame. Carefully pass the blade through the pin hole in the two pieces. Secure the lower end into the lower chuck of the saw. Create light tension on the blade by gently squeezing together the two arms of the saw frame. Tighten the upper chuck while the two arms are still squeezed together. Release the arms very slowly.

Cautiously move veneer pad and saw until the blade comes very close to the throat of the V-notch in the bird's-mouth. Gently

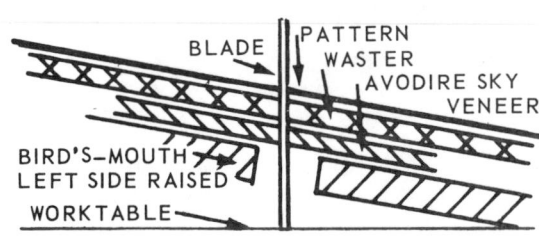

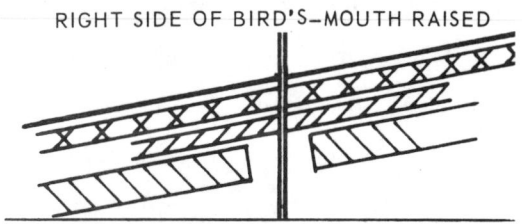

RIGHT SIDE OF BIRD'S-MOUTH RAISED

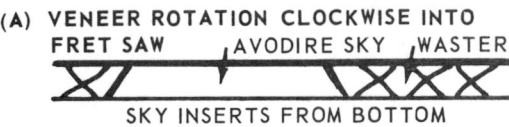

(A) VENEER ROTATION CLOCKWISE INTO FRET SAW
SKY INSERTS FROM BOTTOM

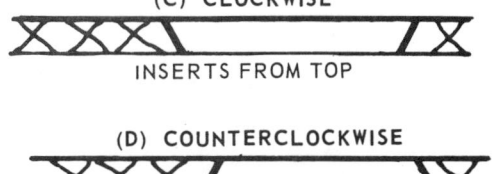

(C) CLOCKWISE
INSERTS FROM TOP

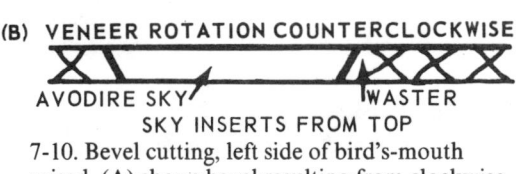

(B) VENEER ROTATION COUNTERCLOCKWISE
SKY INSERTS FROM TOP

(D) COUNTERCLOCKWISE
INSERTS FROM BOTTOM

7-10. Bevel cutting, left side of bird's-mouth raised. (A) shows bevel resulting from clockwise rotation. (B) counterclockwise rotation

7-11. Bevel cutting. Raising the bird's-mouth at right side reverses the beveled joint

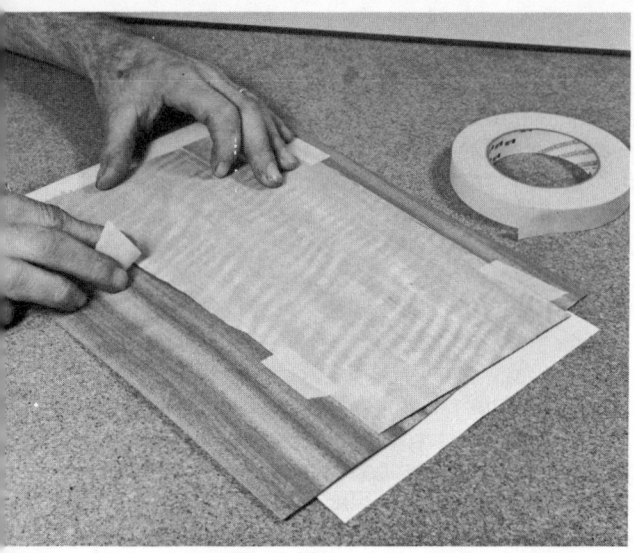

7-12. Veneer for sky taped to back of oversize waster. Sheets will be bevel-cut simultaneously

move the saw up and down in about a 1 1/2" or 2" stroke while keeping the blade vertical. (7-14) Do not move the saw forward, sideways or into a turn. Move veneers into the saw blade. This technique calls for close concentration for awhile but soon becomes ingrained habit.

Place to one side the two pieces you have just now cut. Remove tape and balance of waste avodire from the back of the waster. Lay waster face down on a flat surface. Squeeze a small amount of white glue around the inside of the hole you cut in the waster. Next, insert the avodire sky veneer into this hole. Tape in place (7-15) and roller it flat. The piece of waster that came out of the opening can be discarded. Wipe off excess glue with a damp rag.

The next element to be cut should be one of the largest remaining elements. The lake

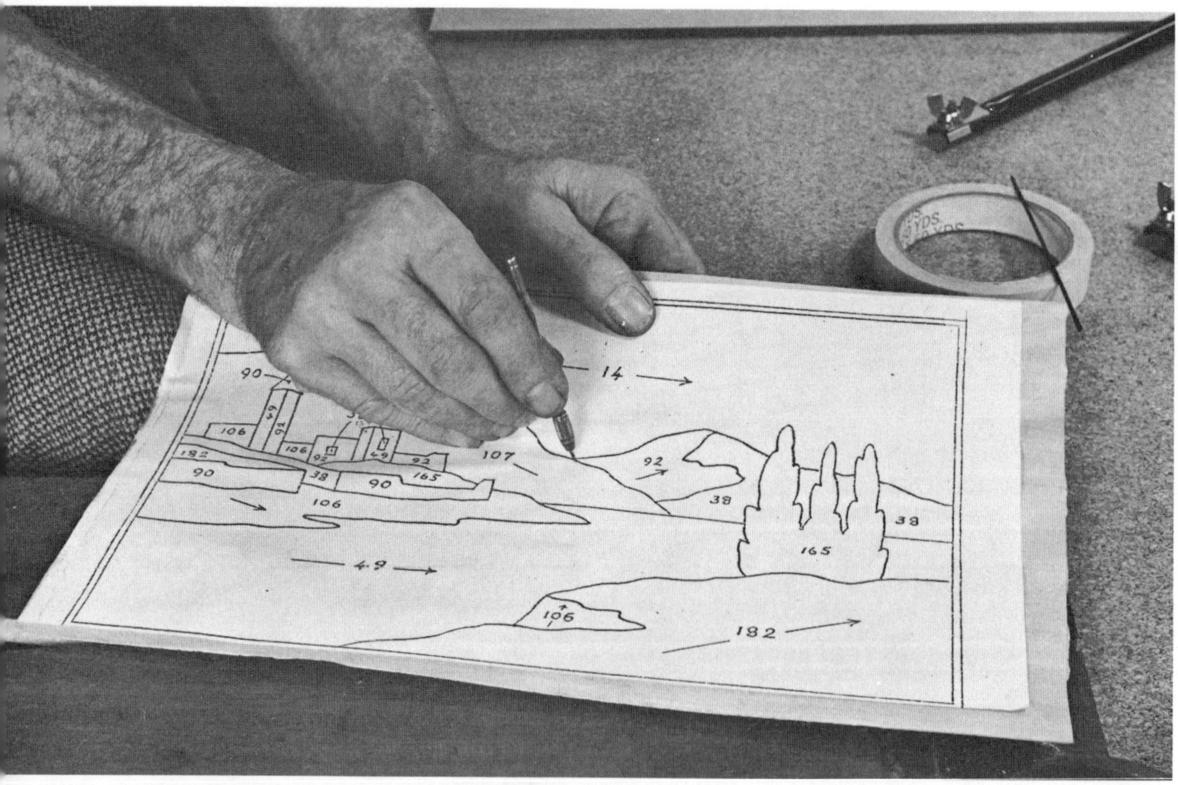

7-13. Needle pierces hole for saw blade at intersecting lines where it shows least in picture

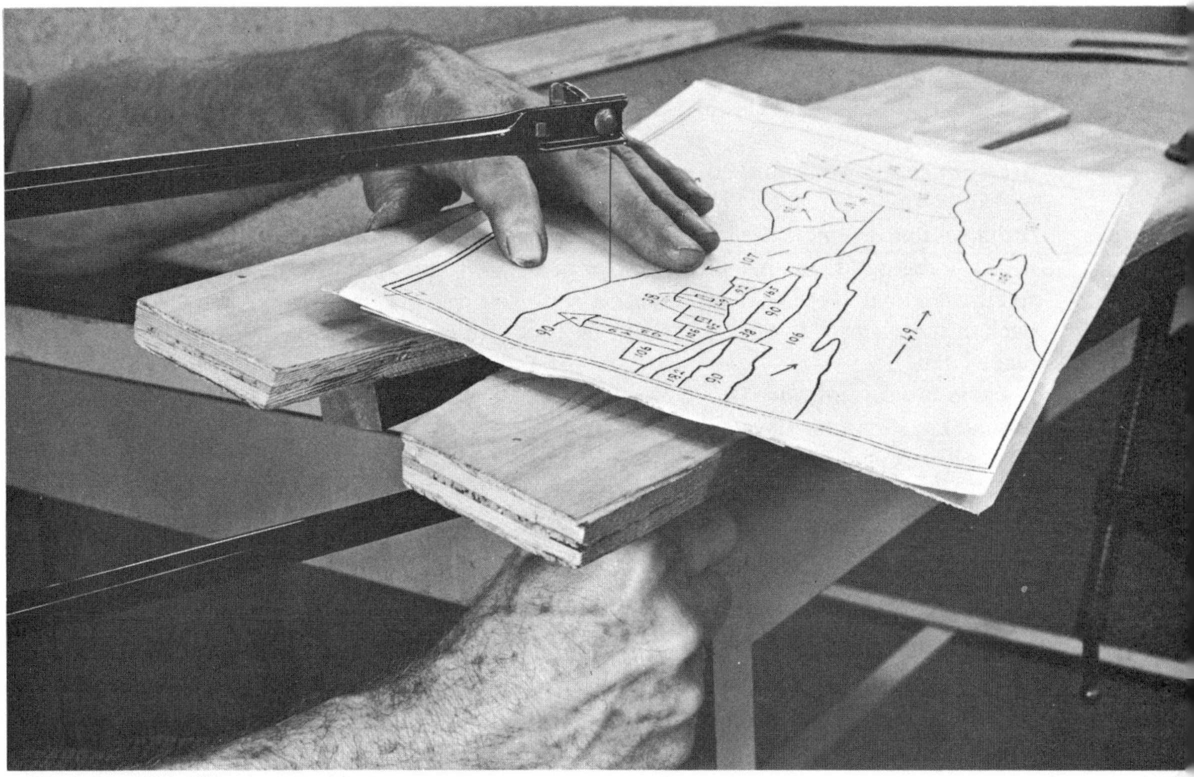

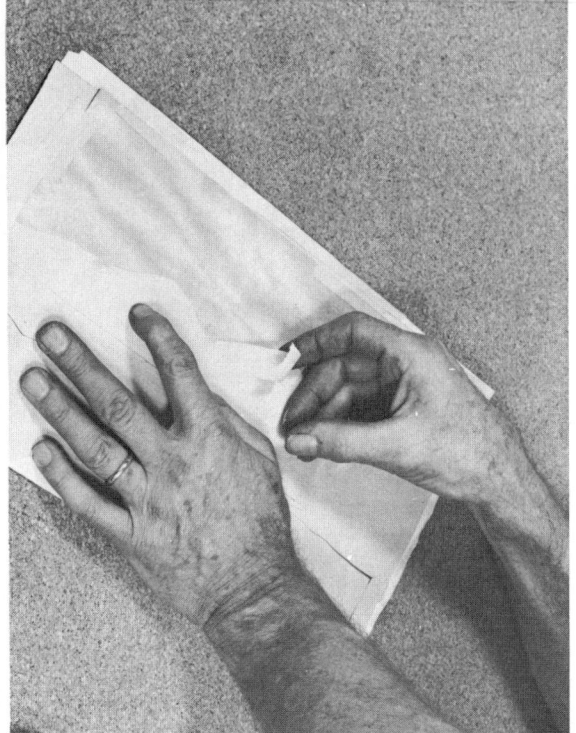

7-14. Work is rotated in one direction on tilted table while saw is pumped in vertical position

7-15. Avodire sky veneer is taped into position in opening made when waster and sky were cut

7-16. Harewood lake cut with waster, ignoring tree clump, is edge-glued and taped into waster

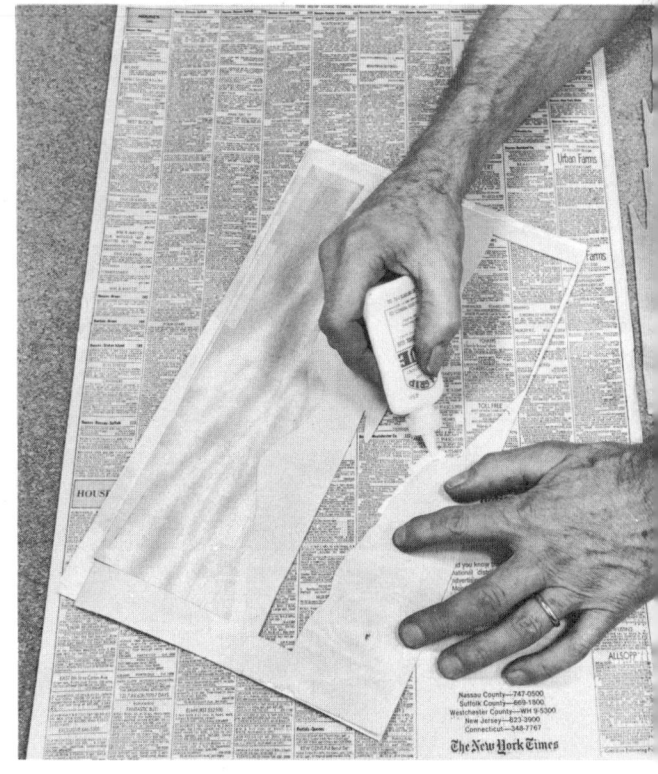

is a good choice. Follow the sky procedure for cutting and assembling it into the waster. When cutting the lake ignore the clump of trees. Cut the lake right through the trees as though they did not exist. Turn the waster over. Squeeze glue around edges of opening and inset the lake veneer. (7-16) Next you could cut and assemble the shoreline plateau in the foreground. In this piece ignore the small triangular piece that represents a setback in the plateau. It will be cut and set in place later.

There are several other basic elements in "Swiss Lake" to be developed before the trees, setback and chalet are considered. Disregard these elements while cutting and assembling into the waster, one piece at a time, the three sections of mountain and the distant shore.

When all basic large pieces are in place, you now use the master pattern. Register it to the work pattern which is still attached to the waster although portions of the pattern

have been cut out. Insert a piece of carbon paper, carbon side facing waster, between the master and waster work pattern. Trace the small pieces that bisect the large areas, such as the trees, chalet and so on. You now have the small elements accurately marked on the veneers that were assembled into the waster. Using these new outlines, cut and insert one at a time the properly selected veneers. Continue this procedure until the entire picture is complete.

Lay a steel square on the completed picture assembly and trim off excess veneers from all edges. If you do not have a steel square use some other means of squaring up the assembly. Trim with veneer saw or craft knife. Most craftsmen prefer the saw.

You can now add borders, stringers or inlay banding around your picture and prepare for mounting. Instructions for various procedures from this point on are given in later chapters.

8. Power scroll-saw method of cutting

Cutting veneer with a power scroll saw has some obvious advantages over knife and fret-saw cutting. It is faster, easier and better. You can follow a pattern line with precise accuracy because both hands are available to guide the work into the saw while holding the veneer firmly down on the saw table. Both the scroll-saw blade and the fret-saw blade have a tendency to lift the veneer on the upward stroke. This is easily overcome when cutting on the scroll-saw table. The scroll-saw blade, furthermore, travels in a grooved guide which prevents wavering. This feature greatly increases accuracy of cut. All kinds of veneer—hard, soft, thick, thin, brittle and crumbly—are cut cleanly without the hazards some of them present to knife and fret saw.

The obstacles to power cutting are cost of equipment, noise and untidiness. The last two objections don't count if you have a workshop or a room separated from family living space.

At this time only one manufacturer is known to offer a power scroll saw suitable for cutting veneer. The maker is Rockwell International, Power Tool Division. The demonstration here was carried out on a 16-inch model which is no longer being made. The current model made by the same manufacturer is a 24-inch model in Chapter five shown before it was adapted to the special requirements of marquetry with the addition of accessories as seen here. (8-1).

It is well to remember that model changes take place from time to time and such changes may require more or fewer adjustments than described here, all of which were

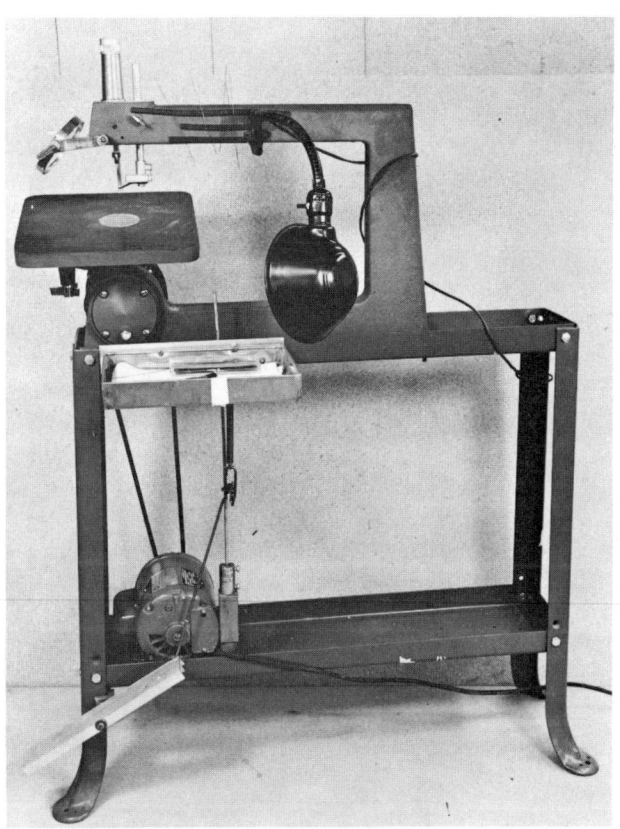

8-1. Whether you own this 16-in. scroll saw or plan to buy 24-in. model (the only one now made) changes for marquetry are about the same

made on the 16-inch model.

Additions to the standard model included saw stand, top and bottom marquetry chucks, saw blade guides, lamp, step pulley and other items offered by the manufacturer. A variable speed model also is now available. The unit illustrated here includes worthwhile adjustments and some im-

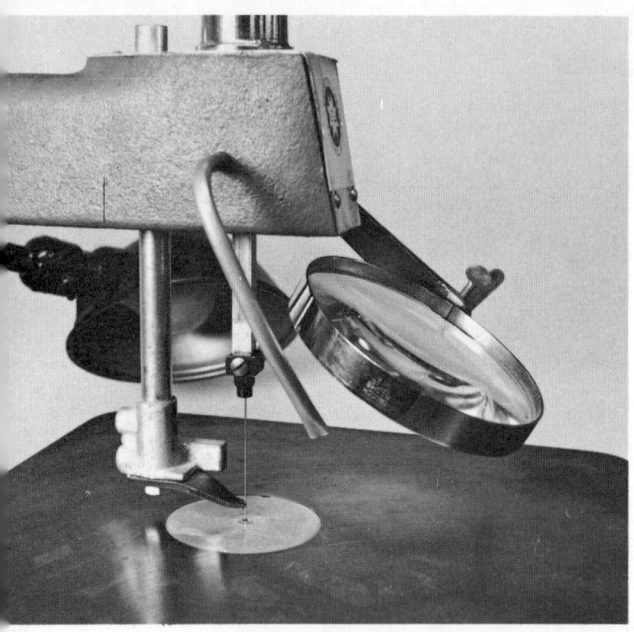

8-2. Scroll saw adapted to marquetry needs has special chucks, new table insert, tool tray, foot switch, magnifier and other changes

8-3. Suspended tube is blower. Special guide steadies blade and holds down the veneer

provised features not readily procurable. For example, blade tension was reduced to lessen blade breakage. Saws that do not have an adjustment for spring tension in the upper housing should be fitted with a spring having less tension. Two or three spirals cut from the original spring will serve as a replacement if a spring cannot be located.

The table insert that comes as a standard fitting with the saw has a large slot which may present problems. Small pieces of veneer can fall through, and the insert also can cause chattering of veneer being cut. Make an insert replacement out of a similar piece of metal. Cut it round to fit the table hole and drill a small hole in the center to pass the saw blade. (8-2). If preferred you could glue a sheet of thin aluminum over the entire table and drill a saw hole in it; or you could simply stick a piece of tape over the opening after threading a blade in the upper and lower chucks.

Illumination at the work area is a must. You can attach a lamp sold for this purpose or devise a means of attaching a gooseneck desk lamp to the saw frame. Attach two or three short lengths of strip magnet to the saw frame as a handy keeper of spare blades.

Another important visual aid is a magnifying glass. It should be attached where it can be focused on the work-point of saw blade and veneer. A 4" round glass with frame and handle can be adapted to the problem. Use your ingenuity in making it functional. You could utilize the two 10-32 1/2" tapped holes in the right side of the saw frame intended for the accessory lamp. Improvise a holder with a combination of thumbscrew, metal bars and rods. The unit has to be adapted to each person's vision.

The scroll saw comes equipped with a blower (8-3) which can be moved to direct a stream of air to remove accumulating sawdust. If you buy the saw stand invert the shelf to provide a tray for containing tools.

A 1725-1/3 hp. motor with 4-step pulleys mounted on motor and saw with a connecting belt riding on the largest pulley on the saw and the smallest pulley on the motor provides a speed of about 650rpm. This is about right for marquetry work. Do not have the belt too tight. It will strain the bushings and wear them out prematurely.

Another practical innovation is a foot-activated on-off switch connected to the motor. It gives instant control of saw motion while freeing both hands to guide and hold the veneer. Commercial foot switches are sold, but are hard to find. The contraption on the demonstration unit is totally satisfactory.

Special self-centering jeweler's blade chucks must be purchased for marquetry. Install them in place of the chucks that come with the machine. This is another must.

To align the blade in the saw, after installing the marquetry chucks, insert a No. 4/0 saw blade into the lower chuck. It is self-centering. Next, lower the top chuck over the top of the saw blade and tighten. With the blade now secured, install the smallest blade guide in the holder. Blade guides are purchased as a set of six with varying widths of slots to take different widths of blades. (8-4) Lower the blade guide holder just above the

8-4. Replacement guides in six sizes are slotted in tip ends to take different widths of blades

table top, then move the blade guide so that the apex of the V-slot just touches the back of the blade. Due to the exacting requirements of marquetry cutting, it is suggested that the blade guard be removed to provide unobstructed vision. Also remove the holddown spring. The blade guide will act as a work holddown during cutting, and you will have unobstructed vision at the point of contact of saw and veneer. (8-3)

The 16-inch Rockwell Delta scroll saw enables you to cut 16" deep or a circle of 32" diameter. By rotating the upper and lower chucks 90 degrees virtually unlimited lengths can be cut. The 24-inch machine permits cuts up to 24" with the blade cutting toward the front and to unlimited lengths when chucks are rotated a quarter turn.

Preparing veneer. The way in which veneers are to be prepared for cutting depends upon each person's preference. The following brief details are intended simply as introductory guidance.

Practically all methods require a drawing or sketch which can serve as a cutting outline. One of the preferred ways is to mount the drawing on the background veneer by applying rubber cement to the back side of the drawing and laying it in position on the veneer. The oversize piece of veneer to be cut and inlaid into the background is then taped into position on back of the background veneer. By holding the pieces of veneer up to a strong light, you can easily determine the correct location.

Threading the blade. Make a small hole through both pieces of veneer, just large enough for passage of the blade. You can use a small pin held in a pin vise for this procedure. Carefully pass the blade halfway through the veneer. Now pass the lower end of the blade through the hole in the table insert and into the lower self-centering chuck. Tighten the chuck. Lower the upper chuck over the upper end of the blade and tighten that chuck. Next, lower the blade guide until it just touches the top veneer.

The above procedure is to be followed even if you use a tilted table, but in that case the table must be tilted before you thread the blade into the chucks. If you are following the bevel-cut method, which requires a tilted table, tilt it to about 12 degrees so that the left side is higher. Use the protractor on the front of the machine to gauge the angle. Lock the table in position.

When all of this has been accomplished turn on your light and adjust the magnifying glass. Check the blade with your finger to see that the teeth are facing forward and pointing down. Assuming that the blade pierces the veneers at a point where two or more lines meet, when that is possible, turn on the power. A foot switch frees both hands.

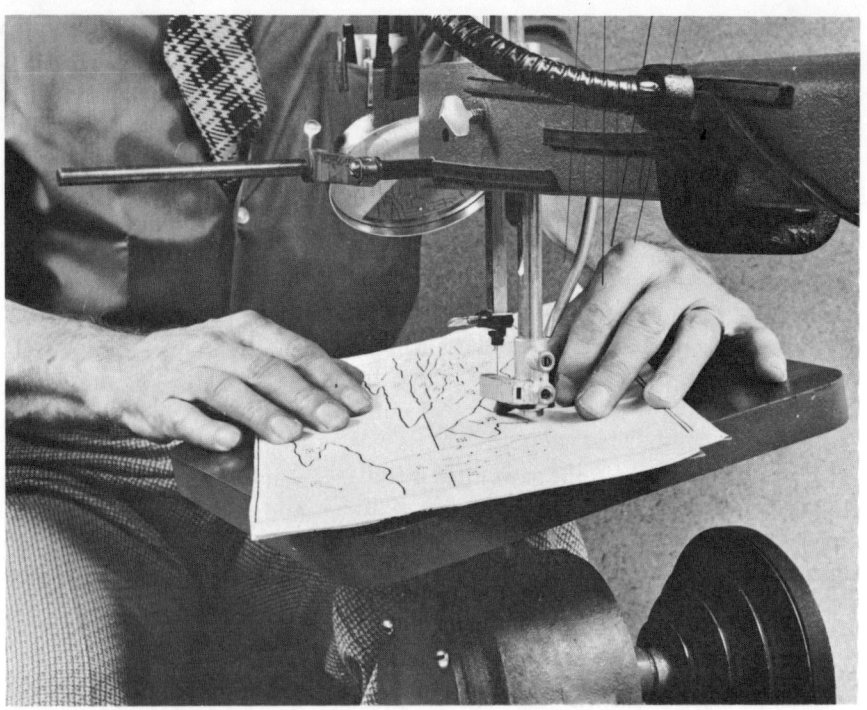

8-5. Bevel cutting. Table raised at left side. Veneer being fed counterclockwise into saw

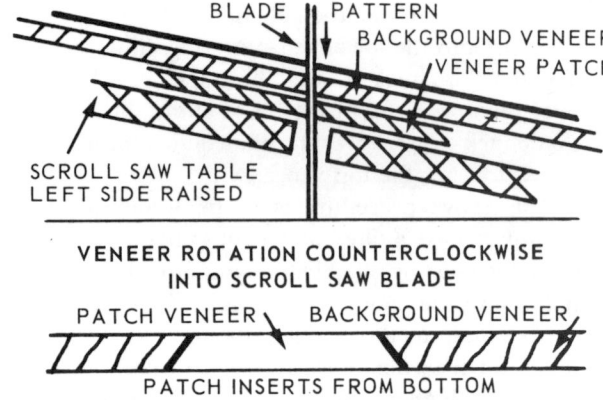

8-6. Cross sections show effect of work feed and table tilt on bevel cut in veneer patch

Cutting. Move the veneers in a counterclockwise direction, feeding slowly into the saw blade. (8-5) Continue cutting until you return to the starting point.

The bevel-cut method on the scroll saw, using tilted table, produces bevel cuts that are opposite to those accomplished with the fret saw. The reason for this turnabout is that the scroll-saw blade cuts toward you as the workpiece is pushed away from you; whereas the fret-saw blade cuts away from you while the workpiece is pulled toward you. Cross-section diagrams (8-6) relate the two factors controlling the bevel: the tilted table and the direction of workpiece rotation into the scroll-saw blade.

When necessary to make a sharp turn while cutting, stop the motor. With your left hand move pulley or belt (8-7) to provide very slow saw movement while simultaneously turning the veneers with your right hand. When you have reached the new direction of the cutting line, turn on the motor. Do not attempt to feed veneers too fast. Do not become discouraged if your first results are not what you hoped for. The more you practice, the faster you will improve.

Assembling cut pieces. At the completion of the cut, raise the blade guide, loosen the top chuck, then the bottom chuck. Remove the blade, being very careful not to lose any pieces of cut veneer. Untape the veneer patch from underneath the background veneer and insert the patch into the background. Use transparent tape on the face.

You will now discover that you have made a perfect fit of patch into background. Even if you happened to stray a fraction from the line, that error is made in both pieces and they must fit perfectly regardless of what happened, because they were cut simultaneously. You may now position your second patch on back of the background veneer and proceed as before. Continue this procedure throughout the entire picture.

At times you will cut away portions of pattern lines needed later. To replace missing lines place a carbon sheet between the mounted drawing and a spare copy of the drawing. Make sure that the copy is in exact alignment with the drawing which you cemented to the background veneer. Trace the necessary lines back onto the background veneer.

Accent lines. Occasionally there are elements of a picture that can be improved by a free-standing accent line; that is, a line that is not connected to other lines. To cut accent lines into the picture first return the table to its horizontal position. If protection or reinforcement is necessary back up the background veneer assembly containing its various patches with a piece of scrap veneer or a piece of index card. Again pierce for the saw.

8-7. Motor off. Making sharp turn. Slow saw action provided by turning pulley by hand

This time perhaps a No. 2/0 blade would be advantageous. Thread the blade and make the cut. (8-8) These accent lines can be filled with colored wood filler or splinters of any appropriate wood.

8-8. Accent lines are cut with saw table flat although other cuts are made on tilted table

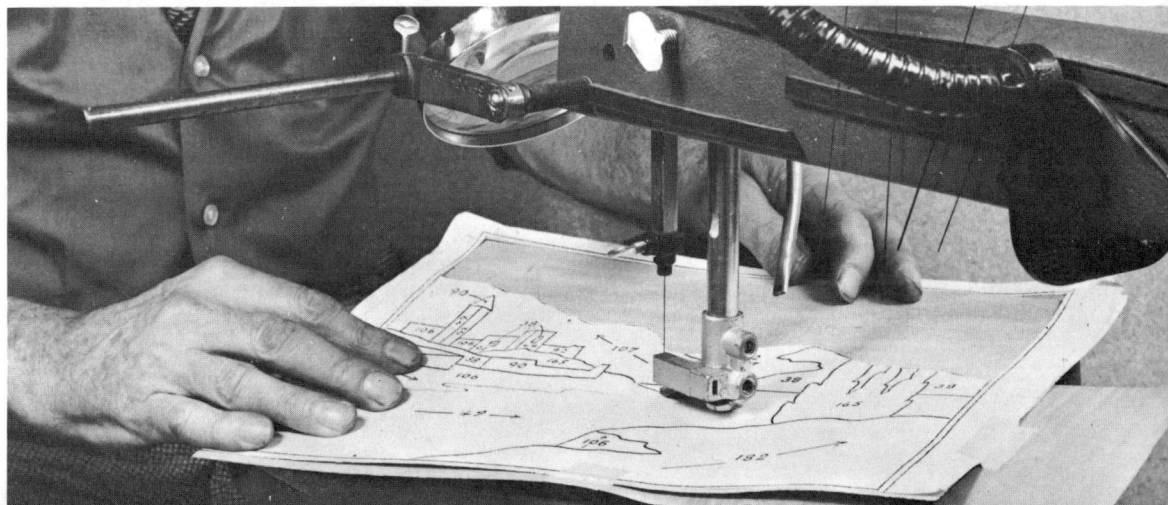

9. Patch-pad method for fret saw and scroll saw

For those who may not be familiar with the marquetry pad, it can be defined as a stack of veneers sandwiched between two blinds, usually thin poplar or basswood because these woods are soft and easy to cut. The technique is still sometimes called the "sandwich method."

With variations the pad method of cutting veneer parts to compose a wood picture has been in use for a very long time. Professionals who make such pictures in mass for sale, break up a picture into kinds of wood and make a pad of many sheets of just one kind. Amateurs are more likely to adopt the simpler, but quite wasteful, method of building the pad with full sheets of five or six

kinds of wood. (9-1) The resulting scramble of cut parts can be assembled into five or six pictures composed of mixed parts, no two pictures alike and only one picture fully acceptable for color and figure.

A more economic method to be explained here is the patch-pad system. (9-2) It involves a considerable amount of preparatory work but greatly increases the possibilities for contrast and it utilizes a minimum of your valuable veneer. The pad can be cut with a hand fret saw or a power scroll saw. For this demonstration an old-time pedal-powered jig saw was used. You can see this genuine classic in Chapter 1.

The principle of the patch-pad method is simultaneous cutting of joining elements of the picture. When joining elements are cut with one pass of the saw blade the two parts will fit together with no more opening than the thickness of the tiny saw blade. To make sure that walnut burl tree foliage, for exam-

TOP BLIND
1/8" BASSWOOD

CEMENT FULL
PATTERN
TO TOP
BLIND

VENEER

BOTTOM BLIND
1/8" BASSWOOD

9-1. Simplest type of pad is made of full sheets of good veneer. Faster but somewhat wasteful

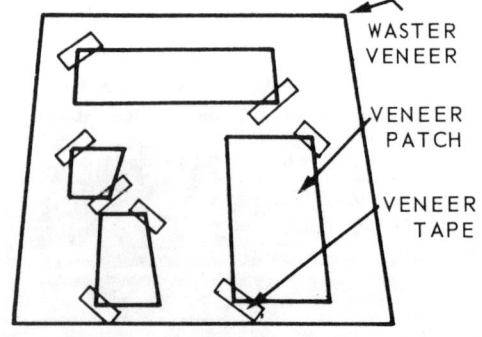

WASTER
VENEER

VENEER
PATCH

VENEER
TAPE

9-2. Patch-pad method uses sheets of low-cost veneer called wasters. Holes are cut in wasters. Patches of good veneer are inset in holes so that each patch is exactly under its pattern area

ple, is cut at the same time as avodire sky surrounding the tree, the patches of burl and avodire must be on different wasters. A piece of walnut burl, cut slightly larger than the outline of foliage, is patched into waster veneer in picture location. Other patches regardless of kind will be patched into the same waster in their appropriate picture locations. A patch of avodire as large as necessary is patched in picture location into another waster.

As with other marquetry methods you need prints of the picture in line drawing form. Top and bottom blinds which will cover the top and bottom of your pad can be made from thin wood, veneer or even cardboard. These blinds should be cut at least 1/4" larger than the picture to allow about 1/8" margin all around. You need some sheets of inexpensive veneer such as poplar or African mahogany (plain) for wasters. A waster is a sheet of veneer, pad size, into which patches of selected veneers are inserted. You may need six or eight wasters. A patch is a piece of veneer selected for a picture element. After various patches have been inserted into a waster, the assembled sheet is called a leaf. Blinds and wasters must be carefully cut to the same size. You need one pattern to go on the top blind and two spare patterns.

After all wasters and blinds have been cut to pad size, number each and mark the edge that goes to the top of the picture. As wasters become assembled leaves you will find it useful to keep a record of patches within the leaf. Also, for insurance, check off on your spare pattern each element as it becomes a patch in one of the wasters.

Sometimes a patch will cover two or more picture elements of the same kind of wood if close together. One or more of these parts can be made as separate patches and moved to another leaf if this will save a waster.

Since there must be enough patches to provide all picture elements, there must be enough leaves to accommodate all patches, but the number of leaves must be kept to a minimum. Pads generally contain from five to eight leaves. More leaves than that can

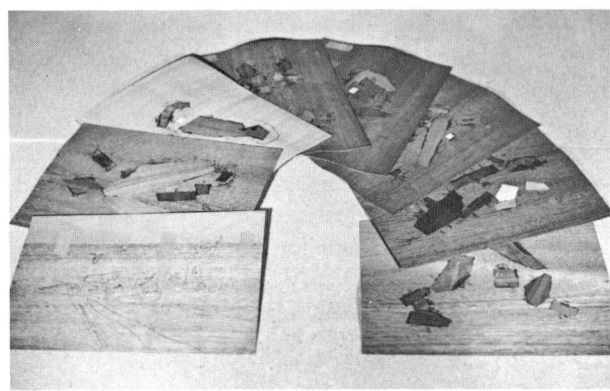

9-3. All leaves except one are wasters containing good veneer patches. Third from left is full sheet of background veneer with central patch

cause frequent blade breakage. Picture size has little to do with leaves required. Large pictures use larger wasters which accommodate more patches.

Various picture parts such as sky, foreground, water, or a combination of these often take up large sections of a picture. A complete waster is not needed here. Simply join a waste piece to selected veneer to make up a full-size leaf. Sometimes the selected veneer for two large parts can be joined to make a full waster. If background veneer completely surrounds the picture the selected veneer serves as a waster with internal parts patched in. The spread of leaves illustrated (9-3) has just such a leaf, the third from the left-hand corner. All leaves are complete except one at lower left which does not yet have windows cut in for patches.

Patch locations must now be drawn on each waster. Lay the cut pattern on one waster. Stick a snip of masking tape at the top edge to hold the pattern precisely in place. With carbon paper and stylus trace onto the waster. Number each patch area to match pattern numbers. If this procedure shows that two adjoining elements of different woods have been assigned to one leaf, one element must be moved to another waster. Repeat this operation for each waster you are preparing.

After initially assigning patches to wasters, a little more juggling generally will show a way to eliminate one waster. Patches no farther apart than 3/8" at the closest point can be assigned to the same leaf. They can be as close as 1/4" if care is taken to cut the pad accurately. When a piece of waste veneer is not wide enough for a full-size waster join another piece to it with veneer tape. Grain direction of wasters is unimportant.

9-4. Leaves sandwiched between blinds. Pattern cemented on top blind. Pad taped tight

Windows are now to be cut in each waster to receive assigned patches. Use pencil and straightedge to outline an area slightly larger than the actual pattern outline. Work one area at a time. Cut the window with your craft knife. Place the piece of selected veneer under the window. Trace this window outline onto the selected veneer. Remove the veneer to a cutting board and cut the patch with your knife. Insert the patch into the window of your waster. Hold it in place temporarily with snips of veneer tape on the up side of the waster.

When all patches have been cut and taped into their properly assigned places on a waster, turn over the assembled waster, or leaf, for glue sizing. Rub a thin film of white glue over each patch and work it into the joints. The glue-sized leaf now goes into clamps or under weights for a short time. Sandwich it between caul boards with a sheet of plastic film under and above the leaf. Later, peel off the plastic film and allow the glue to air cure. After the glue has dried, cover the patches on the glue side with veneer tape, taking care to butt edge the veneer tape. Do not overlap the edges of veneer tape. This is the reverse side of the leaf, the underside in the pad.

Gluing and taping is simpler and more important than it may sound. It greatly reduces the common problem of losing or breaking delicate parts during the sawing operation. Glue strengthens the veneer while tape on the underside gives more support than it would on top. The layer of tape remains through the cutting and assembly operations and is removed only after the face side has been taped, at which time you are about ready to glue the entire veneer assembly on a mounting panel. Sizing the patches solves another occasional problem. It eliminates ooze-up through open-pore woods if you glue your picture to a mounting panel with white or yellow glue. Contact glue causes no ooze-up when properly applied.

At this point snips of tape on the top side of the leaf, placed there to hold patches until secured with glue, must be removed. If veneer tape was used it must be dampened for removal. It is advisable to keep all leaves under moderate weight when not being worked.

Assembling the pad. Mark the two blinds for top or bottom and identify the edge of the top blind which will correspond with the top of the picture. Assemble the leaves into the pad with top edges aligned. Although you numbered the leaves you need not assemble them in that order. It is good practice, however, to separate leaves having a lot of small patches in the same area. Pay close attention when padding up and double check to see that all are right side up and top edges aligned. To reduce the bulge that usually occurs at the center of the pad, you can put just a spot of white glue here and there on wasters, providing you put it where it won't run to a patch when the pad is compressed. Spot gluing between every other layer is enough.

Bring all leaves into precise alignment. Have a few strips of masking tape pre-cut. Beginning at the center of one edge, compress the pad tightly and bind with tape. Do the same on the opposite edge. Finish taping all around the pad every inch or two.

Align the picture pattern on the top pad and attach with rubber cement. Clamp the assembled pad with moderate pressure for overnight. (9-4)

Sawing the pad. A closer fit can be made with a 6/0 blade but breakage could be frequent. A 4/0 blade is acceptable and less frustrating. The picture must be drilled or pierced with a needle at all internal parts which cannot be reached when you saw from the edge. Always pierce in a corner or at a point where there are intersecting lines. Do the piercing as you go along, when ready to saw the area.

Saw internal parts first except for extremely small parts which are sometimes left until last. Occasionally it is practical to cut tiny parts out of the cut-up pad and saw them separately. To do this you take the piece of waster the part is in, the piece the part goes in, and the corresponding sections of blind. Hold these pieces together with tape or rubber cement. Pierce this little pad and saw to the outline which is still cemented to that section of top blind. This practice gives you a thinner pad to saw and facilitates part removal.

The best place to start sawing is at one corner if you will not be cutting into background veneer. Before making any cut, plan the sequence and direction of cuts. It would be a mistake to cut all edge pieces before cutting some interior parts. As cutting progresses put snips of masking tape on the cut edge of any part of the pad not yet sawed.

When a picture is too large to start cutting at a corner follow a line from one side to the other somewhere through the picture. Tape edges of separated sections. Where background veneer completely surrounds the rest of the picture, you can cut the picture proper without background and assemble it, then knife-cut a window in selected background veneer to receive the central assembly.

Separate the pieces after cutting each part. Some of the waste pieces have been spot-glued, but never the usable parts unless you made a mistake. Place all cut picture parts in shallow boxes unless you prefer to assemble them on a pattern as you go along. Waiting until all parts are ready has the advantage of allowing more choices for adjustments. Save waste pieces for possible later use.

Picture assembly. You can follow your favorite method of assembly or build the picture face up by laying cut parts on your duplicate pattern. Use snips of veneer tape to hold parts together. Make necessary adjustments as the assembly progresses. If a piece is missing go back to the waste pieces you saved, find a matching piece of veneer and cut a new piece. Sometimes the wrong piece was saved and your scrap box will yield the right one.

After the veneer assembly has been completed, lay veneer tape over the entire face. Tape will be removed after mounting. Never use masking tape for this purpose. Turn the assembly over and remove all tape from the back. Keep the entire assembly flat under weights at all times when you are not working with it.

From here on follow standard procedures for trimming, adding borders, filling, sanding, mounting and finishing. As with other marquetry methods, there are optional ways to work with the patch-pad method. When you discover a way best for you, adopt it.

10. Veneer borders for marquetry pictures

Marquetry pictures do not necessarily need a surrounding veneer border. Most pictures seem to hold together visually a little better when finished off with a border. Pictures that are set into a background that extends to the edge of the mounting panel, such as a sailboat surrounded by sky and water, look very well without veneer borders. Your individual artistic judgment should be your guide in determining whether a border should be added.

If you elect to add a border there are many options. The simplest border is made of four veneer strips measuring from about 1/2" to 1" wide laid flat on the mounting board to surround the picture. Marquetry pictures are seldom framed with conventional picture molding but occasionally you will see one

handsomely framed. Grain of the veneer border customarily runs the long way of each strip, but short-grain strips are often seen. Fancier borders include the intricate herringbone style illustrated (10-5) with cutting procedure for you to follow.

Very often an interrupter border measuring about 1/8" wide is used. It is a very thin strip of veneer fitting between the picture and the wider border. These interrupters are called stringers or fillet borders. Black stringers are high favorites, but any contrasting veneer can be cut into narrow stringers. Black strips as well as satinwood and rosewood are available for this purpose in widths of 1/16, 1/8, 3/16 and 1/4 inches. Also there are readymade inlay bandings (10-1) made up of contrasting woods in many designs and

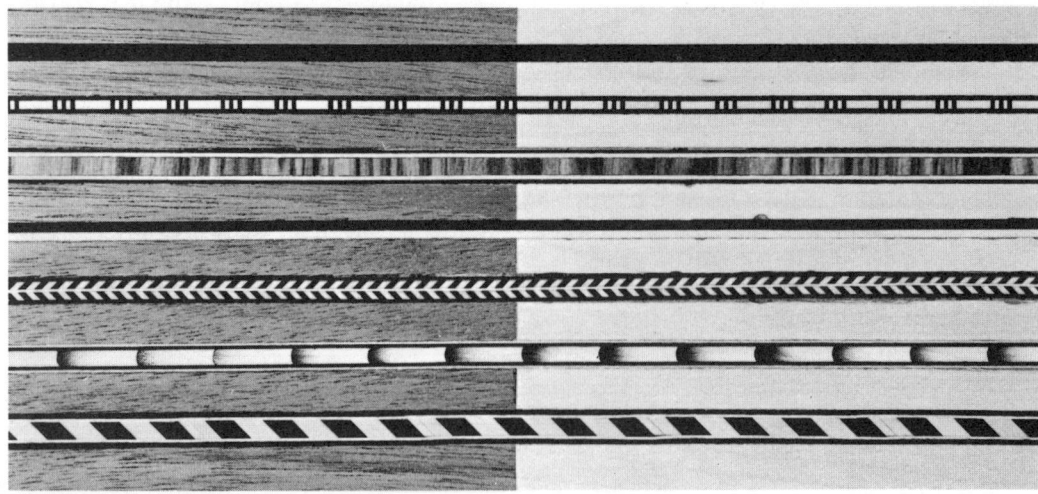

10-1. Narrow stringers used to separate picture and veneer border offered in attractive styles

10-2. Use a square, a straightedge and a knife to square and trim four sides of picture assembly

widths. One of these decorative stringers was chosen for the marquetry picture used in the accompanying bordering demonstration photographs.

Start the bordering procedure by carefully squaring off your picture (10-2) to the desired size. Use a 12-in. steel square or a combination square. Trim off the excess with a veneer saw or a craft knife. Select the veneer you are going to use as border. Cut strips in uniform width and long enough to surround the picture with allowance for overhang. Make certain that the ends overlap 1/4" or more. If you are including stringers inside the wide border prepare them now by cutting a contrasting veneer to required width and length. If readymade banding is to be used, cut it to length. Allow extra for overlap at the corners. Use veneer tape or transparent tape to hold stringers and border tight against the edges of the picture. (10-3) Tape goes on the face side of the picture. Check to see that these added strips are tight against the picture and that ends overlap.

To cut the miter joints select any corner to start on. Using your steel straightedge accurately line up the point on the outer edges

where the borders intersect and the inner point where the stringers intersect. When these points are lined up hold the straightedge firmly in place and make light cuts with your craft knife. Always cut from the outside intersecting point to the inside intersecting point. (10-4) Take extreme care not to cut into the picture. When both pieces of border and both pieces of stringer have been completely cut through remove the cutoffs and tape together the miter cut that you have created. Continue this procedure at all four corners of the border.

Another technique for bordering is sometimes followed. In this method borders are not pre-trimmed to width. Start this procedure by using the steel square to square and trim the picture. Then tape four strips of wide border veneer around the picture, allowing ample overlap at the ends. Draw layout lines on the border strips at the exact width you want the final border. Use this layout as a guide in cutting your mounting board. Lay the cut mounting board on the veneer assembly and mark each corner on the border. Lay a straightedge so that it aligns with these corner marks and the cor-

87

10-3. Tape long stringers and border strips to protected face of the picture before mitering

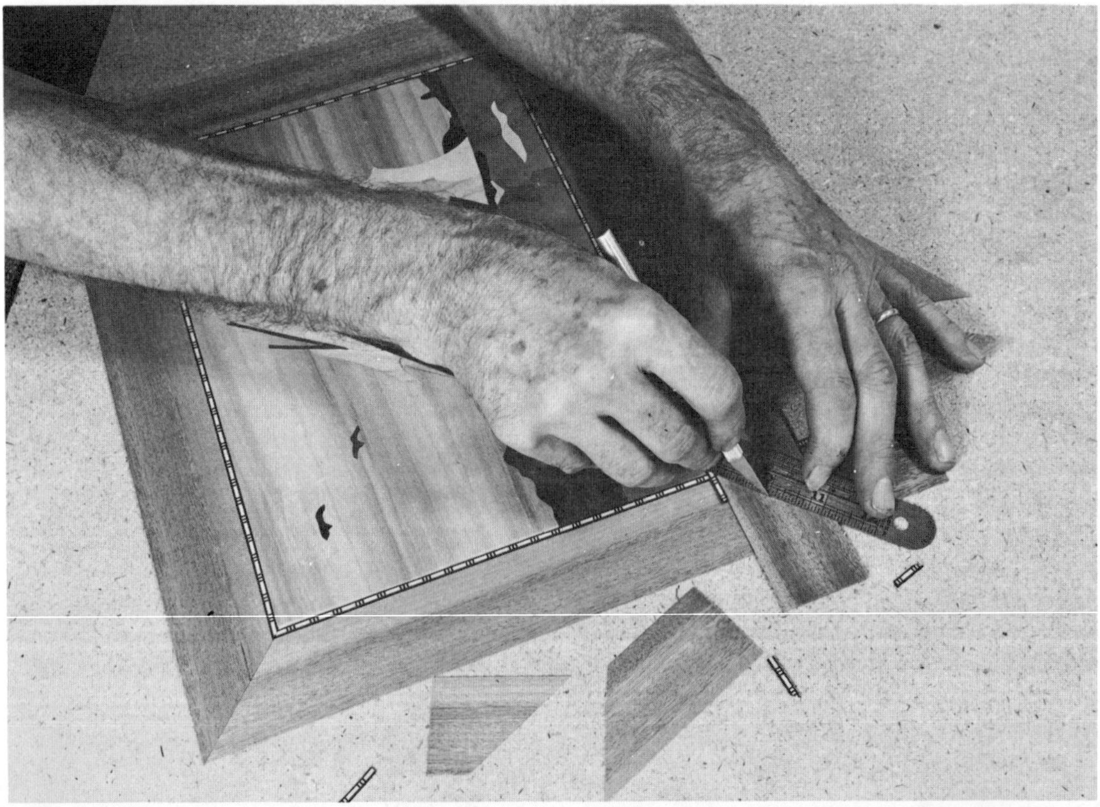

10-4. Align straightedge with outer and inner intersecting points. Knife-cut toward picture

ner of the picture. Cut against the straight-edge to make a mitered corner. This method provides a final-size mounting board and an oversize veneer assembly which will be trimmed flush with the mounting board after mounting with glue.

Herringbone border. Sometime you may have a special marquetry picture that could appropriately be displayed with a border more decorative than straight-grain or short-grain strips. The herringbone design should be considered. It's a lot more work but time limitations should not always be applied to craftwork.

The illustrated procedure is based on a 7 x 9 picture to be laid with stringers and border on a 9 1/4 x 11 1/4 mounting board. The final border will be 1" wide. Straight-grain veneer is basic to this design because the grain of flopped alternating strips must form the visual angle that makes the herringbone pattern. Walnut was used for demonstration.

Start by tracing the outline of the mounting board on a larger cutting board. (10-5 A) Remove the mounting board. Either tape or edge-glue stringers to the picture. Center the picture with stringers attached within the traced outline. Now trace around the stringers. Remove picture. Draw vertical and horizontal centerlines as well as corner diagonal lines. Diagonal lines will assure exact miters even if the picture is slightly out of square. Replace mounting board on outline and carry centerlines across the mounting board to provide a centering guide for final gluing of picture to board.

Cut a strip of walnut veneer 3" wide. Length depends upon picture size. For this demonstration two 18" strips are just about right. One long strip would be awkward to handle. This amount will produce the fifty-two short diagonal strips needed here plus a few extra for insurance. Cut off the end of one long strip at 45 degrees. Then cut diagonal strips 9/16" wide (B) making the cuts parallel with the cut end. As diagonal strips are cut, line them up in their original location except for turning over every other strip. (C) This procedure creates the right-angled grain effect you are striving for. Don't expect to have even ends from this assembly method. Ends will be trimmed when necessary.

For assembly place picture on cutting board within its outline. Start at the lower left corner. Align No. 1 strip with the diagonal layout line and with one end flush against the stringer. (D) Edge-glue it in place. Trim the end of No. 2 strip and edge-glue it in position. Make certain that the strips extend at least 1/2" beyond the mounting board outline. They can be trimmed after the entire picture assembly has been glued to the mounting board. Continue this procedure until you have covered border area just past the vertical layout line. (E) Place a

3" STRIP OF STRAIGHT—GRAIN VENEER
GRAIN DIRECTION
9/16 STRIPS

CORNER DIAGONAL LINE
CENTER VERTICAL LINE

WASTE
45° CUT

CENTER HORIZONTAL LINE
MOUNTING BOARD OUTLINE
PICTURE AND STRINGER OUTLINE

STEP A   **STEP B**

10-5. Herringbone outer border made of walnut veneer strips can be cut and assembled as shown

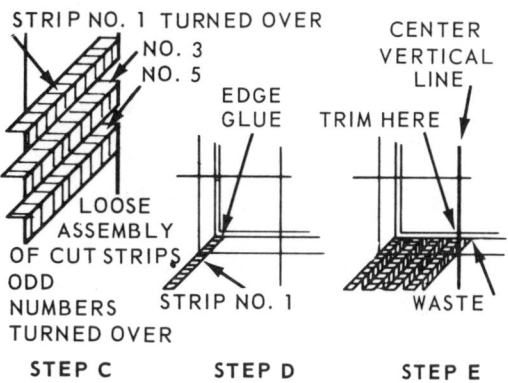

STRIP NO. 1 TURNED OVER
NO. 3
NO. 5
LOOSE ASSEMBLY OF CUT STRIPS ODD NUMBERS TURNED OVER

EDGE GLUE

STRIP NO. 1

CENTER VERTICAL LINE
TRIM HERE

WASTE

STEP C   **STEP D**   **STEP E**

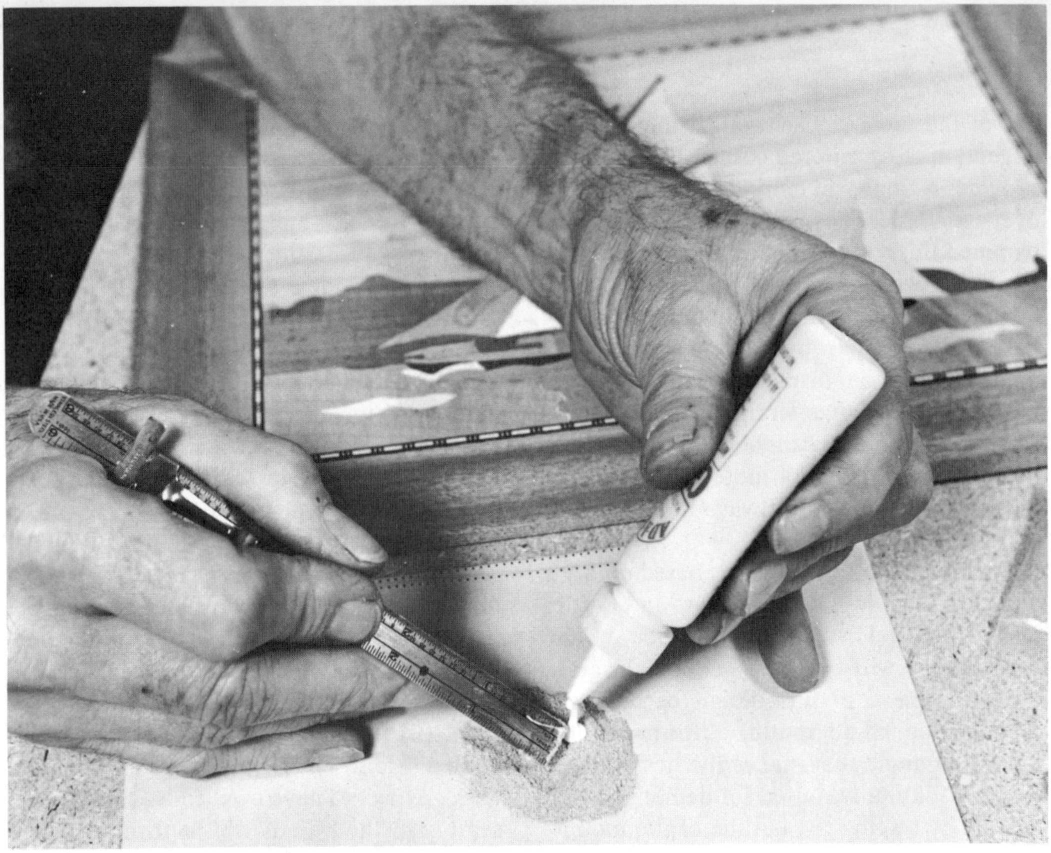

10-6. Even the experts fill joints with sawdust and
white glue mixed to form workable paste

10-7. Fill back of picture. Force sawdust and glue
mix deep into all cracks and tiny holes

straightedge on the vertical line and trim excess herringbone border strips with a knife. Return to the first strip and work your way up to the horizontal centerline. Repeat this method for remaining corners. Start at a corner each time and work toward the centerline. Make a neat centerline joint.

Before removing tape holding picture in position on the workboard be certain that completed border areas are taped to the workboard to prevent shifting.

Filling and scraping. Preparation for mounting is carried out in the same way whether or not borders have been added. The first step is to cover the face side of the veneer picture with veneer tape to hold the assembly safely together. Face tape will remain until after mounting. Next, remove all tape from the back. Filling joints is to be done on the back side.

Hold the assembly up to a strong light to locate any small holes or imperfect joints or accent lines purposely cut through the veneers to indicate lines such as branches of a tree overlapping other branches. Any such openings must now be filled with space filler.

Space filler is a powder which may be purchased commercially or can be prepared when you need it. By preparing it yourself you can make up small batches to match, or at least come close to matching and blending with veneer in the picture. Choose a scrap of veneer and scrape it with your veneer saw or a single-edge razor blade until you have a small pile of sawdust sufficient for the job. Don't use sandpaper to make sawdust. You'll create more silica dust than wood dust. Mix the sawdust with white glue to the consistency of heavy cream. (10-6) Use only white glue for this purpose.

Do all filling on the back side. Spread the mixture of glue and sawdust into all cracks and holes. Use a spatula or a scrap of flat metal to force the mix into the bottom of

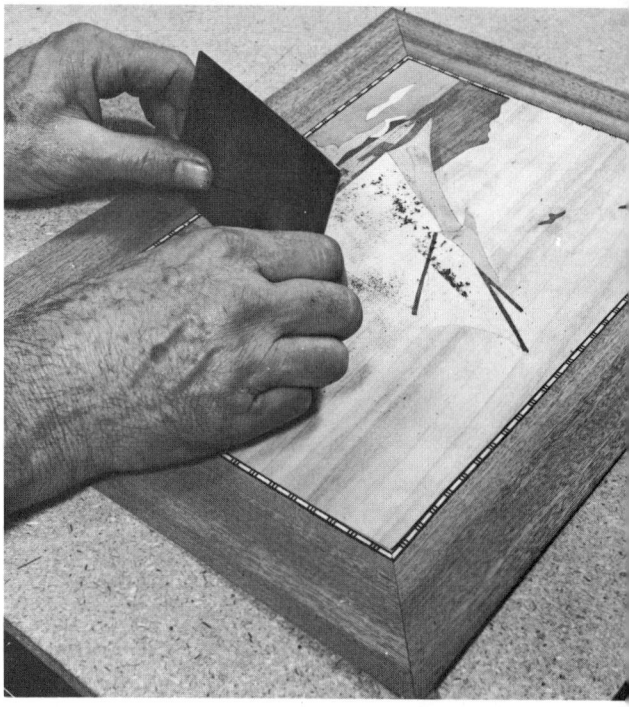

10-8. Remove excess filler and level assembly by scraping back surface with cabinet scraper. Keep this important tool sharp. See how, Chapter 18

cracks. (10-7) You cannot avoid smearing the mix beyond cracks being filled, but this is the back of the picture and will be hidden when glued to a mounting panel. Remove excess filler by scraping the entire back surface with a steel straightedge or a cabinet scraper. (10-8) Lay a sheet of wax paper or plastic over the back surface and place the assembly between boards and under weights for overnight.

At this juncture it is advisable to leave the assembly for a few days under weights. This interlude allows it to dry and gives you a chance to check it a few times to view it critically. Inspect it carefully. Examine workmanship on details. See if you have left out any element necessary to the story idea of the picture. And see if you want to take something out. This is your last chance to make corrections and improvements.

11. Mounting methods for pictures — adhesives to use

All veneer assemblies must be mounted on a stable backing panel. The type of material you select for a mounting panel and the type of adhesive you choose can affect the permanence of your marquetry creation. Give careful consideration before making a decision on the basis of using what you happen to have on hand.

Panels. Particle board makes a good mounting panel. It is smooth, stable, resistant to humidity changes and it cuts cleanly to provide chip-free edges. Be sure to buy smooth, high-test particle board. Low-test boards are rough and have nicked edges. Smooth-surfaced plywood is acceptable if thick enough. Fir plywood should be avoided because the irregular surface is apt to telegraph through your veneer picture and give it an uneven surface. When using plywood lay the predominating grain of the picture at a right angle to the outside plywood grain. Solid wood should never be used as a mounting panel. It will warp when subjected to the stresses of applied veneer.

Small pictures in the range of 4 x 5 usually can be mounted safely on 1/4" plywood without danger of warping. Pictures in the 6 x 8 range are safer on 3/8" thickness, and larger pictures should go on 1/2" plywood. Particle board of 3/8" thickness is suitable for all sizes up to 18 x 18 and possibly larger. Particle board should always be veneered on the back to balance the face picture.

The size of panel required in relation to your picture is variable; that is, at the time for mounting it can be the same size as the picture, larger than the picture or smaller than the picture.

Glues for mounting. There are quite a few different types of glue that can be used to adhere your veneer assembly to a baseboard or panel. However, a survey among marquetarians showed that three types are the most popular. (11-1) This report does not imply that other types are unsuited to the purpose. The declared preferences, not necessarily in the order of preference, are: white glue which sets slowly and requires overall clamping; yellow glue (aliphatic resin) sets fast, makes a stronger bond than white glue and requires overall clamping; contact glue, or contact cement, requires no clamping. Be sure to avoid water-soluble contact cement. It will curl the veneer before you can lay it on a panel and will blister after being laid. Repeating: do not use water-soluble contact cement on veneer.

Two types of glue described here require clamping. Inadequate clamping will cause edge-lifting and blistering. Whatever devices you use to apply pressure to glue-fresh mounting assemblies must provide overall pressure. The first requirement is a pair of equal-size caul boards. One of the best is particle board which you can obtain as cutoffs at most dealers in building materials. Then you need solid crossbearers to reach across the glue-up assembly and exert pressure on central areas. You need either handscrew clamps or C-clamps to put pressure at the ends of crossbearers. Angle iron makes a good crossbearer. It does not flex or bow at the center and it can be used with smaller C-clamps than required for equally rigid wood crossbearers.

A dependable glue-up assemblage consists

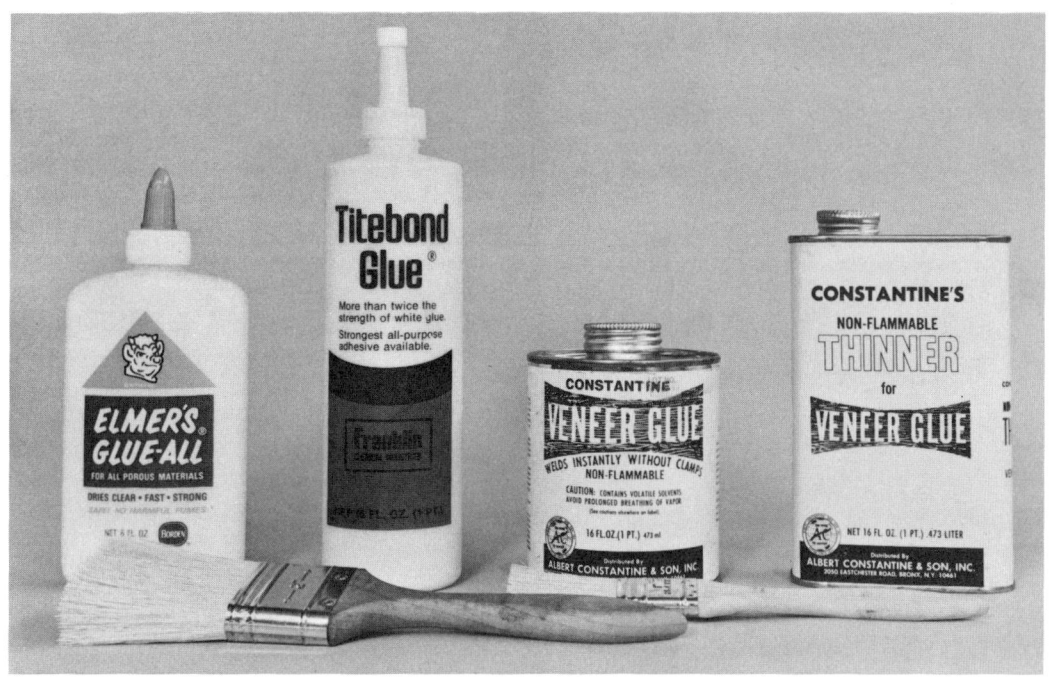

11-1. White glue, yellow glue and contact glue are types most frequently used for mounting marquetry work on a stable panel. Contact type is becoming the favorite among marquetarians

of two cauls, four angle irons, four C-clamps and brown paper, wax paper or sheet plastic to go over and under the picture and mounting board. (11-2) Paper keeps glue squeeze-out from adhering to the cauls. Brown paper absorbs some of the moisture which leaves the glue during drying. Practice varies in the use of paper in a glue-up sandwich. Wax paper and sheet plastic are least likely to stick to the glue. A few sheets of newspaper are usually added but never touching a picture.

Veneer presses were abundant before the advent of modern glues and better clamping methods. They are large, cumbersome, expensive to build and are not now considered essential unless production quantities of large marquetry pictures are being made.

Veneering sequence. The order you follow in mounting is somewhat a matter of individual choice, but it also depends upon the relative size of picture and mounting panel. Briefly, these are the options:

1) if the veneer picture is larger than the panel, the picture is laid and trimmed; the

11-2. Good setup for glues requiring clamping. Angle iron, C-clamps, particle board, paper

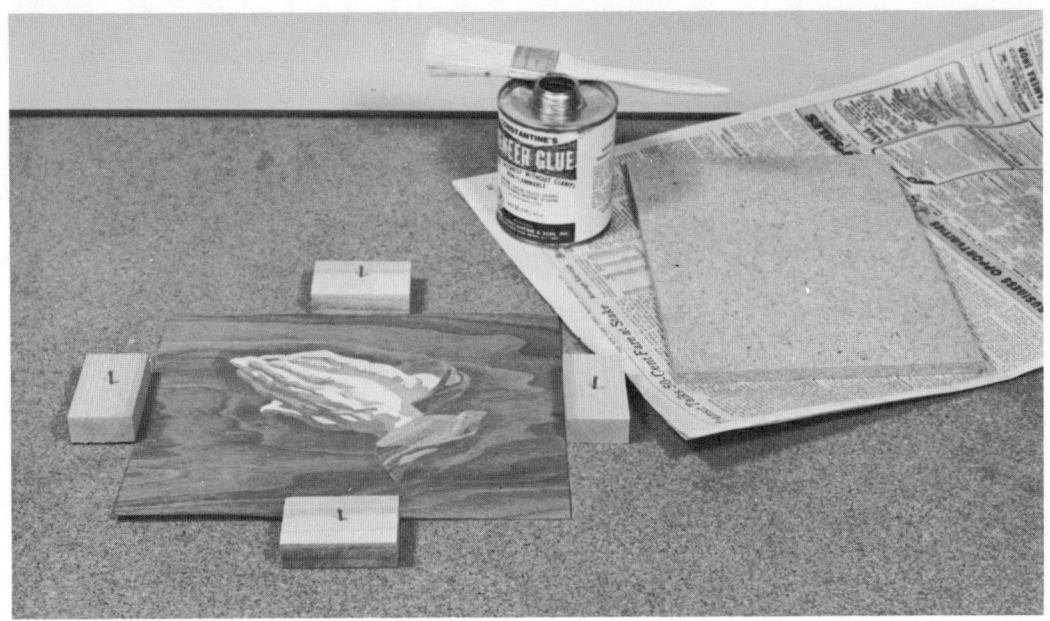

11-3. Four wood blocks nailed around picture
form accurate guide for the mounting panel

11-4. Contact glue on picture and panel bond at
once when panel is lowered within guide blocks

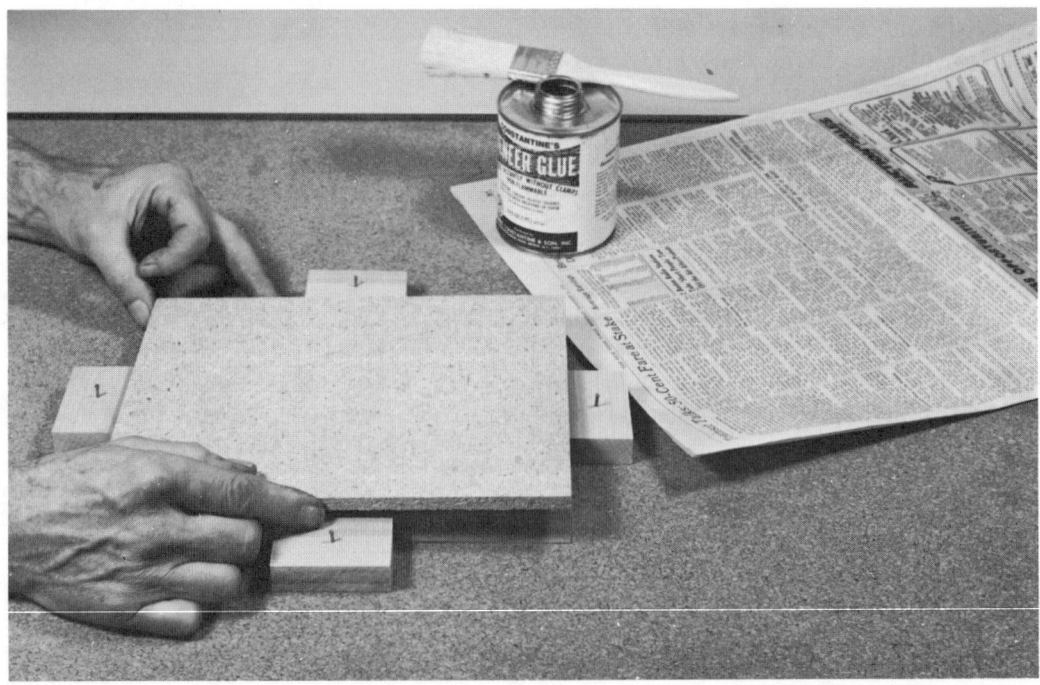

back is then laid and trimmed; and then the edges are veneered and trimmed.

2) the above procedure can be reversed; that is, back laid first if desired.

3) if veneer assembly is larger than panel, edges can be laid first and trimmed before the oversize back is laid and trimmed; and then the oversize picture is laid and trimmed.

4) if picture is undersize, lay picture; trim panel to picture size by using a circular saw or hand file. Lay oversize backing veneer; trim backing veneer. Lay edging; trim edging. Veneer only one edge at a time.

5) if picture is exactly same size and aligns perfectly with panel, lay picture. Lay oversize backing veneer; trim backing veneer. Lay and trim edging.

6) if picture is same size as panel, you can lay edging first; trim edging. Lay picture or backing panel next.

7) if yellow glue or white glue is being used to lay picture that is same size as panel, both the same-size picture and the oversize backing veneer can be set up in cauls and clamps at the same time to save 24 hours waiting time over glue-ups done separately.

8) if contact glue is being used, lay one element at a time. Determine the best sequence by following applicable instructions above for oversize, undersize or same-size picture.

The assembly sequence you are to follow must be determined early enough to have the veneer assembly and the mounting panel large enough for your chosen procedure. The sequence you follow in gluing picture, edging veneer and backing veneer is a matter of choice. Some experts like to have the picture large enough to cover edging veneer. To achieve this effect the panel must be cut to final size and edging applied ahead of the face. Usually, however, if veneers selected for edging are the same as the borders, it is difficult to detect which was applied first.

Regardless of the type of glue applied to the panel, it is advisable, except in the slipsheet/contact method, to lower the panel perfectly flat, not tipped, onto the picture assembly. When picture and panel are the same size nail four guide blocks on your work surface. They must touch all four edges

of the picture. (11-3) Use extreme care in lowering the panel within the guide blocks and onto the picture. (11-4) This method avoids the possibility of cracking or breaking veneer edges which can happen when the alternate system of laying picture on panel is followed.

Guide blocks can be used also when an oversize picture and a final size panel are being glued. In this situation the veneer backing, as an example, is laid on the work surface. The mounting panel is laid, without glue, on top and in position. Blocks are held against the panel and nailed to the work surface right through waste area of the veneer. (11-5) Waste area is trimmed later.

If you are using white glue, and to a less extent faster-setting yellow glue, you have a

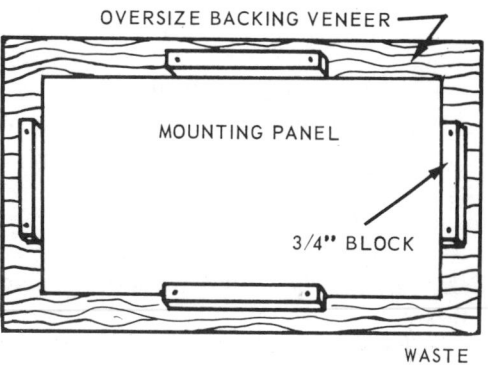

11-5. Mounting jig for oversize veneer. Blocks for guiding panel are nailed through waste veneer

moment's opportunity to slide the assembly slightly to improve alignment. With contact glue there can be no shifting. With white and yellow glue you need a clamping setup.

No matter what sequence you are following, the basics are the same. Start with a clean, smooth, uncrowded work surface. Apply white or yellow glues only to the mounting panel, not to the veneer picture. Set in clamps for 24 hours.

After applying pressure inspect the edges for glue squeeze-out. Wipe away the glue with a damp rag, not a wet one. When the assembly comes out of clamps dried glue remaining at edges can be removed with a veneer saw or a single-edged razor blade. Any necessary trimming of overhanging veneer or projecting panel should now be handled. After that a sheet of veneer can be applied to the back. Thin panels especially need a backing sheet to balance whatever warping tendency may be exerted by the veneer picture on the face. Backing veneer probably is good insurance for every panel. To save 24 hours of extra clamping time backing veneer can be applied at the same time as the picture, providing the assembly will not come out of clamps with two veneer lay-ons extending. Trimming two at a time is too risky. Edges may now be veneered if not accomplished earlier.

Contact adhesive. As more marquetarians hear of the advantages of contact adhesive—quicker, stronger, easier to clean up at edges, and now non-flammable—this glue is becoming the high favorite. If you are starting marquetry without a shopful of clamping equipment you, too, will appreciate the economy and the convenience of contact adhesive. When properly applied contact adhesive makes a strong, blister-free permanent bond.

Work rules for contact are different. Fairly strict, in fact. First, the terms contact adhesive, contact cement and contact glue—as used in this book—are interchangeable. They mean the contact-type of product. The precautions and work rules mentioned here are for your early consideration and future guidance.

1. DO NOT use water-soluble contact adhesive. It will curl, warp and crack any sheet of veneer it is applied to. The water content first expands the veneer, then shrinks it as water evaporates.

2. For safety sake be sure your contact adhesive is non-flammable as recently required by law.

3. Follow manufacturer's instructions on the container. Don't rush drying time of the adhesive applied to your veneer and panel.

4. If thinning of the adhesive is necessary use the manufacturer's recommended thinner. It is chemically compatible. This thinner can be used also for cleaning your adhesive applicator. A type of contact adhesive called Veneer Glue is recommended. It is a rubber-base, non-flammable, non-staining contact adhesive which, within the experience of many marquetarians, has been time-tested and proved to be dependable for use on veneer.

Before applying glue to any surface be sure to mark the gluing surface. Near the top edge of veneer and panel put a penciled X to signify glue side and aligning edges. Number all strips of edging and number corresponding panel edges.

Briefly, the basic contact gluing procedure is to apply two light coats of glue to both surfaces that are to be bonded. Two light coats are recommended. Veneers and panels are porous. The first coat is absorbed into the pores of veneer and panel. Approximately 60 minutes after applying the first coat you can apply a second light coat to both surfaces. Wait the recommended time, usually 40 to 60 minutes. However, experience has shown that an additional wait of 30 minutes after the second coat significantly increases the bonding strength. Any further wait is likely to reduce the bond. DO NOT allow two coated surfaces to touch until you are ready for mounting. On contact, as the product term implies, the surfaces will bond together for good. You don't have a second chance to align your work.

Test for tackiness. After you have applied glue and have allowed the proper waiting time, test the surfaces with a piece of brown paper. Lay paper on the glued surface and apply gentle finger pressure. If the paper does not stick the glue is ready for bonding. Even though the paper does not stick, the two glue-spread surfaces will bond instantly if they touch. Keep them far separated until you are ready.

The thought of misalignment may make you hesitant to work with contact, but careful adherence to the following instructions will assure success. You can follow any of several methods for accurate and safe mounting.

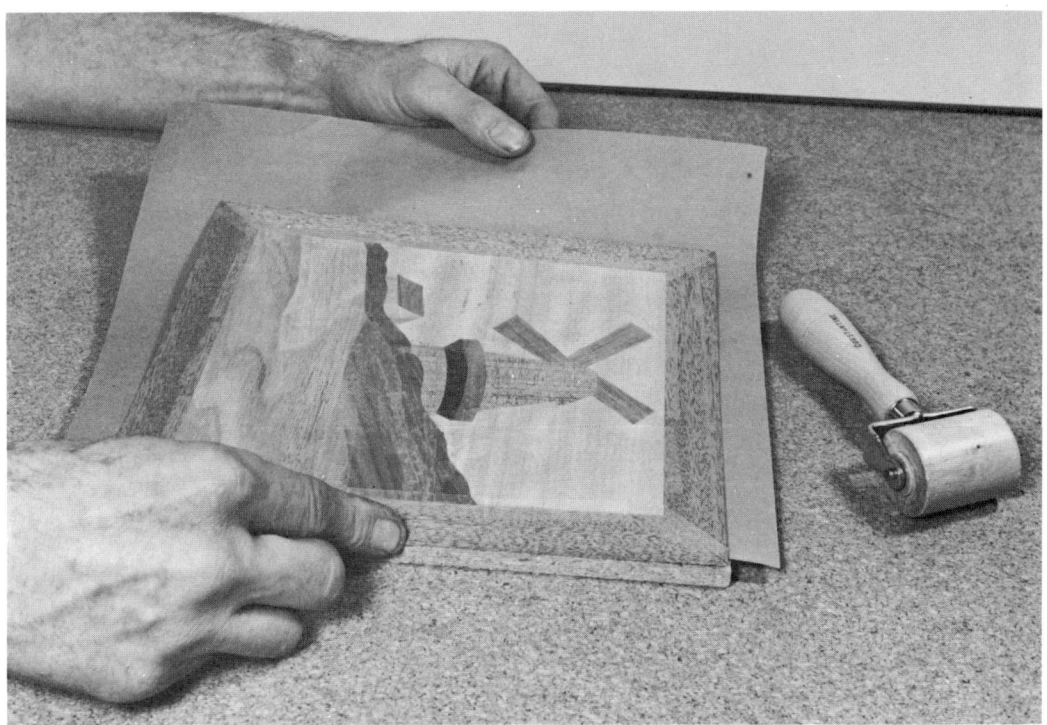

11-6. Paper slipsheet separates two contact-glued surfaces until slowly withdrawn after alignment

The size relationship of veneer picture and mounting panel, which you have determined before you reach the gluing stage has a major bearing on how you proceed with mounting. Was the panel cut to final size before gluing? Do you intend to apply edging veneer first? With these options predetermined you are able to select one of the following bonding methods.

Slipsheet method. This is a way of keeping glued surfaces apart while you are establishing perfect alignment before bonding. An oversize piece of brown paper bag or a sheet of wax paper can serve as a slipsheet to separate the surfaces. This demonstration (11-6) using the simplified version of "Windmill" assumes that the veneer assembly and panel were cut to the same size before glue was applied. When the two surfaces have passed the test for tackiness lay the panel in front of you, adhesive side up. Place a slipsheet over this surface, allowing about 1/16" along one panel edge exposed. Gently lay the veneer assembly in position so that the veneer aligns

perfectly with the exposed edge of the panel. Avoid hand pressure on the veneer picture. Pressure will make the slipsheet harder to withdraw. When alignment is satisfactory gently tap along the 1/16" exposed surface to start the bonding at that edge. Recheck alignment. Slowly pull the paper from between the two surfaces while applying moderate pressure with your hand or a veneer roller where the surfaces are being exposed by withdrawal of the slipsheet.

After the slipsheet has been completely removed apply pressure to the entire surface. Use a veneer roller or go over the surface pounding a small, smooth block of wood with a rubber mallet. Or you can sandwich the assembly between two caul boards and place in a vise for a few minutes. After initial contact and pressure no further curing or pressure is necessary for a permanent bond. Backing veneer can be applied to the panel now in the same manner. Take extra care when applying contact glue to other surfaces. Keep the face veneer free from glue drop-

97

Above, rollering is one good way to apply overall pressure on face veneer laid with contact glue. Below, another pressure system. Smooth wood block moved around and pounded hard with rubber mallet

pings. And be sure to spread out fresh newspaper often during the gluing operation.

If you elected to make veneer assembly and backing veneer larger than your panel you can still use the slipsheet method with a variation. Alignment is the problem. To overcome blind alignment you can pre-trim one edge of the veneer picture to final size. This system gives you one edge to align with the panel while still using a slipsheet. After bonding you can readily trim overhanging veneer with veneer saw or craft knife. Always trim overhang before veneering any other surface. Edging, too, can be applied with a slipsheet.

Guide block method. Four small wood blocks make an assembly jig for assuring good alignment of picture and panel. (11-3) This device mentioned earlier in this chapter can be used to excellent advantage in contact gluing. Two variations of the guide block method will be explained. The first assumes that the panel and marquetry picture are the same final size.

Prepare the jig in advance. Cut at least four blocks of wood about 3/4 x 1 x 2. Lay your veneer assembly, gluing side up, on a flat board. Drive finishing nails to attach one block along the top and another along one side of the veneer. Leave enough nail projecting for easy removal. Lay the panel on top of the veneer in proper position for bonding. Nail the other two blocks snugly against panel and veneer edges. Adjust blocks as necessary until you have a good fit all around. Now the assembly to be glued is in secure position and in alignment. Remove both members from the jig and place them on a flat surface for glue application. When they are ready for bonding place the veneer in the jig first, adhesive side up. Then carefully lower the panel (11-4) into the jig, adhesive side down. Tap the panel to force it flat onto the marquetry assembly in exact position. Take the glue-up assembly out of the jig and follow earlier instructions for applying pressure.

The second usage for the aligning jig assumes that you are working with a final-size panel and an oversize veneer picture or sheet

of backing veneer. Make the jig before applying glue to either member. Lay the panel in position on the gluing side of the veneer. Trace around the panel with a pencil to create assembly guidelines on the veneer. Remove the panel. Lay the veneer on a flat board with guidelines showing. Place one guide block on the top guideline and in the area of waste veneer which will be trimmed later. Nail the block. Nail a second block on a side guideline. Lay the panel back in position on the picture, aligned with the guidelines. Nail remaining blocks on guidelines to form a snug fit against the panel. (11-5) The jig should be tight enough to require a light tap to force the panel in position when members are being bonded. With the panel removed, cover inside edges of each block with masking tape. Tape will be removed prior to bonding. Meanwhile it keeps contact glue from covering the edges of the blocks that touch the panel.

You now have the marquetry veneer anchored in place with guide blocks. The panel is set aside. It is time to spread contact glue on both members. Follow gluing and drying procedure already explained. When you are ready to bond remove masking tape from blocks. Lay the panel on the marquetry veneer. Tap in place. Remove nails from blocks. Trim veneer overhang.

The guide block system can be used in the same way when you add backing veneer and edging veneer, although it may not be worth setting up for edging. Even for backing veneer you can get along without guide blocks if you use extra care and if you cut the veneer oversize to allow at least 1/8" at all edges. Pencil guidelines should be drawn on the backing veneer to show exact position for the panel when you are bonding the two. Edging is quite easily laid flush on one edge by simply guiding it with your fingers while withdrawing a slipsheet as you go along. Overhang is readily trimmed off the other edge.

Always remember to trim overhang from one edge before applying veneer to another surface. Take precautions to keep sawdust and wood chips off surfaces coated with glue, and especially contact glue. When removing foreign fragments you are apt to pull up glue as well.

You have seen a variety of methods for mounting your valued marquetry assembly. The choice is yours. Do not be afraid to experiment when you think of an innovation. If in doubt try it out on scrap pieces. Observe instructions on glue containers as well as cautions related here. Use proper thinners. Allow sufficient tacking time. Don't rush. Plan every step ahead. Keep your work surfaces clean. Brush them frequently. Work patiently and carefully. The rewards will be more than worth your extra time.

12. How to finish marquetry work

The veneers you have used in your picture are beautiful in their natural state. They are colorful and interestingly figured. No two look alike. And now that the picture has been mounted on a panel and bordered you may be eager to get some finish on it. Finishing—professional finishing which you will be guided through in this chapter—will greatly enrich the colors and accentuate the figures. A quickly conceived finishing procedure, on the other hand, will deprive your patient handiwork of deserving admiration. At this point, as a matter of fact, your picture is not yet ready for finishing. The most important part of finishing is preparation. And before you undertake it, set the picture aside for several days to allow mounting adhesive to fully set and harden.

Preparing the surface. Remove tape that covered the picture from the time it was completely assembled until it was mounted. If it is veneer tape, as it preferably should be, moisture is required for removal. Use a damp sponge to moisten, not soak. Work on one small area at a time. Something like 8 to 10 square inches. Wait a couple of minutes for absorption. Peel off the loosened tape with your fingers and with the help of a spatula. A sharp knife would damage the veneer. Again set aside the picture to dry out under brown paper, a flat caul board and adequate weight.

A day or two later is the time for minute inspection of the face to see if all cracks have been properly filled. Earlier you applied filler from the back. There may be some joints or tiny holes that were not completely filled to the surface of the face side. Fill them

now with a mix of sawdust and white glue. Work cautiously this time to avoid smears on the face side.

Next check the entire surface and edges for evidence of imperfect bonding. Run a roller over the surface. If you hear a faint snapping noise feel for a blister. The snap indicates a raised area of veneer called a blister. Imperfect bonding of glue makes the snapping sound. There are two main causes: inadequate glue coverage or insufficient pressure or rollering. Blisters can occur with any of the three types of glue—white, yellow and contact.

Remedy for veneer blisters. Lay a piece of aluminum foil over the · blister. Using a household electric iron at moderate heat make several passes over the foil. Heat softens glue if there is any glue beneath the blister. Immediately roller the area fairly hard. Repeat the ironing technique a couple of times. If the blister returns try to force glue beneath the area. Pierce a needle hole in the blister and use a glue injector to force white or yellow glue through the hole. Never mend with contact even though you used it to lay the veneer originally. Apply finger pressure to the blister to spread the glue and force excess glue out through the hole. Wipe off excess glue with damp cloth. Cover the area with wax paper and a block of wood. Clamp and set aside for 24 hours.

Leveling the picture. Surfacing is accomplished with coarse grit sandpaper or a hand scraper. This valuable tool is nothing more than a piece of thin, somewhat flexible tempered steel measuring 3 x 5. When sharpened correctly and maintained in super-sharp

Remove veneer tape from mounted marquetry face.
Moisten small area. Use spatula or sharp chisel

condition, and when properly used, the hand scraper can eliminate a large measure of initial sanding. It cuts rapidly and efficiently, bringing an uneven surface of veneers down to one level.

When sanding or scraping keep the picture level and steady. Nail wood strips to a workbench against top and bottom edges of the picture to wedge it in place. They should be as wide and as thick as the mounted picture to keep it from shifting and to prevent dipping when your sanding block or scraper reaches an edge. Never allow corners of the scraper blade to dip. They could gouge the veneer. Be sure to round off scraper corners with a mill file. To sharpen the scraper properly, follow instructions in Chapter 18. This is one of the oldest tools in the cabinetmaker's toolchest but overlooked too often in these times. Only light sanding with fine grit paper is necessary after a veneer surface has been leveled with a hand scraper.

If you are going to use only sandpaper for leveling your picture, first examine the picture to determine its lowest point. Some veneers are thinner than others. This lowest point is called the caution point. Sand only in one direction and this must be in the direction of predominating grain.

Prepare a sanding block from hardwood such as maple or birch. Cut it 3/4 x 3 1/2 x 5 1/2. This size takes a quarter sheet of standard sandpaper. The block should be smooth on all surfaces and sharp at the edges. The widest face of the sanding block will abrade the high areas and ride over the valleys to bring the surface down evenly. Use No. 80 grit paper until you reach the caution point. Change to 6/0 (220) and then to 7/0 (240) grit. Follow the same procedure for smoothing the back. Lay a sheet of clean brown paper under the face when sanding the back. Don't use newspaper. Sand veneered edges last. This calls for close attention. Keep the sanding block as flat as possible to prevent rounding the edges. Excessive pressure on the block does not increase the cutting speed.

When sanding a picture containing colored veneers use moderate pressure to decrease the chance of rubbing darker colors into lighter areas. Application of a thin coat of sanding sealer prior to sanding reduces the possibility of runs.

Cleaning the picture. Remove all traces of sanding dust. It is good practice to use a vacuum cleaner with a bristle brush attachment.

Finishing tools and materials include several grades of sandpaper, sanding block, clear varnish, brush, cabinet scraper and burnisher for keeping it sharp, and tack cloth for cleaning surfaces being finished.

ABRASIVES used in marquetry

Flint paper. About the only thing to be said for this paper is that it is cheap. It is usually 9 x 10 inches and is graded extra coarse, coarse, medium, fine, extra fine. Not recommended for marquetry. Cannot be used in a machine sander as the paper it is put on is not strong. It wears out and clogs up rapidly.

Garnet paper. This paper costs more, but does more. Less expensive in the long run. Can be used in a machine sander as well as with a sanding block. It is reddish in color and recommended for marquetry.

Aluminum oxide. About the same as garnet but it lasts a little longer. Brown in color and is excellent for finishing hardwoods.

Silicon-carbide. Excellent before putting on the final coat of finish and for rubbing down. It is black in color and very tough. Can be used with water or oil. (Water for varnish, oil for shellac.)

Steel wool. Good for rubbing last coat of varnish. It comes in four grades. Number F0000 should be used for marquetry work.

Pumice. Good for rubbing down when a smoother shiny finish is desired. Comes in four grades. 4/0 is the finest and is used for rubbing down last coat. May be used with water or oil.

Rottenstone. Does no cutting of the surface, but gives a higher shine. Used mostly with oil, but can be used with water. It is very messy.

Rubbing and polishing compound. Does the same as rottenstone, but easier to use and less messy.

GARNET PAPER

Use	Grit	Grade	Description	Back
Leveling	80	1/0	Very coarse	D
veneer	100	2/0	Coarse	C
(Be careful)	120	3/0	Coarse	C
Before	150	4/0	Medium	C
sealing	180	5/0	Medium	C
Between coats	220	6/0	Fine	A
of finish	240	7/0	Fine	A

SILICON-CARBIDE

Before final	320		Fine	A
coat and	400		Very fine	A
final rubbing	500		Extra fine	A

Letters after the grit number designate the type of backing:

A — light paper
C — heavier (also called cabinet paper)
D — heavier than C
E — tough backing, mostly for belt sanders
J&X — cloth

Never go from a coarse to a fine paper in one step. Always coarse, medium, fine and very fine.

Polishing materials: rubbing oil, pumice powder and rottenstone. For satin sheen or high-gloss finish

Next wipe the picture with a tack cloth to pick remaining dust out of wood pores. This is an important part of finishing marquetry pictures because of the many minute joints and pinholes. Tack cloths may be purchased or made at home. To make one start with a piece of cheesecloth two feet square. Wash it several times in tepid water and wring it out slightly to prevent dripping. Apply turpentine liberally and shake out the cloth to lose excess turpentine. Sprinkle varnish freely over the cloth and wring out. Unfold and wring out again. Repeat several times, unfolding and wringing out. The cloth should remain sticky enough to pick up dust but dry enough so it does not ooze moisture when pressed. Store your tack cloth in a glass jar with a tight cap. Occasionally open the cloth and shake it. Add turpentine and varnish when necessary. A tack cloth lasts indefinitely if properly cared for.

Preparation of the surface explained up to this point applies to all marquetry pictures regardless of the finish you intend to apply. The picture is now ready for finish. There are numerous manufacturers of suitable products. And several types of finish to choose from. The two types to be covered here are varnish and French polish. In the hands of the non-professional who lacks ex-

perience and equipment, varnish finish is likely to produce the better result. With practice French polishing also can accomplish excellent results.

Brief description of popular finishes

Shellac. One of the oldest types of finishes. It was used mainly on furniture years ago. Museums that display antique furniture give proof of its beauty and long-lasting qualities. Shellac is fast drying, but not water, alcohol or heat proof. Three to six coats that have been thinned down with denatured alcohol and applied every two hours with light sanding in between can be used for a finish on marquetry pictures. Be sure fresh white shellac is used. A final rubbing with steel wool or pumice and oil will give a mellow finish.

French polish. Combination of shellac, alcohol and oil applied with a pad made by wrapping a piece of clean linen around a ball of waste cotton material or cheesecloth. This mix is applied by rubbing in a figure eight movement until the desired amount of finish is applied. Requires a lot of practice.

Oil varnish. Slow drying, contains natural resins, linseed oil, turpentine and a drier. This type of varnish is being replaced by the newer synthetic varnishes which are faster drying.

Four-hour or plastic varnishes. Fast drying, contain synthetic resins such as Bakelite, alkyds and polyurethane. Chinawood oil as the vehicle and volatile thinners such as varnalene. Wood-Glo falls in this category.

Rubbing varnish. Contains more resins than oil, permitting the finish to dry hard for extensive rubbing when a smooth high luster is desired.

Spray lacquer. Fast drying, contains nitro-cellulose and resin gums plus a variety of other chemicals. Finish is very clear and several coats can be applied in an hour or two. Not recommended for the amateur because a well ventilated area away from spark or flame is required. It is highly volatile and takes some experience in operating the spray gun.

Brushing lacquer. Dries in about two hours. Works well over small areas. Good ventilation away from spark and flame also required. Deft is a popular brand name.

Penetrating oil finish. Applied with a rag or brush. Resistant to water, heat, alcohol and scratches because it penetrates the wood. Two or three applications are sufficient.

Aerosol spray cans. Available in varnish or lacquer spray cans. Dries fast. Recommended for small areas especially miniature doll house furniture, wood pendants and small novelties.

Marquetry finish used extensively today consists of two coats of fresh, white shellac thinned with an equal amount of denatured alcohol and several coats of Wood-Glo with a final rubbing with pumice and rubbing compound. This produces a smooth satin finish. For a little gloss follow with Pledge furniture polish.

Pure varnish is rarely used today. Most varnishes now are made with synthetic materials. They probably are better than pure varnish. Polyurethane varnish is one of the most popular. Wood-Glo, widely used by marquetarians, is a dependable polyurethane varnish.

Varnishing stand. Make a simple drying stand to support the work and enable you to apply finish to all surfaces at one session. In a piece of scrap wood or plywood measuring perhaps 15" square for 10 x 12 pictures drive three finishing nails through the board to project about 1 1/2" on the upper side. Position the nails to form a triangle, all points exactly the same height. This three-point stand supports the marquetry panel. The closer the nails come to edge of the picture the better.

Varnish finish. Stirring varnish just before using it is not advisable. Stirring causes bubbles. A better way to mix is to shake the container vigorously the previous night. About a half hour before varnishing place the can in a pan of hot water. Heat lowers viscosity and makes the varnish flow more freely from the brush. This makes a more even coat.

The recommended brush for varnish is ox hair bristle of good quality. With care it will last a very long time. Nylon brushes are not advised for varnish. The varnish you select should be clear, non-yellowing type. High quality varnish will enhance the beauty of wood. Sanding sealer makes a good first coat. It stops suction, or absorption, of succeeding coats into the wood. A wash coat of white shellac reduced with alcohol is another satisfactory first-coat finish.

Brush a first coat on the back of the picture. Lay the picture on its back side on the nail drying rack and coat the face, then edges. Brush away all runs. Apply only thin coats and allow ample drying time, at least 24 hours. Impatience can spoil a finish.

When the sealer coat has dried thoroughly, lightly sand all surfaces to remove accumulated dust. Use 7/0 (240) finishing paper. Again clean the panel with a vacuum brush and tack cloth.

Apply a coat of varnish. Leave for 24 hours. Sand lightly with 7/0 paper. Clean all surfaces just as you did before, with vacuum and tack cloth. Apply additional coats of varnish, sanding and cleaning between coats, until you have established an even surface. This may take from three to fifteen coats. As you sand between coats using the flat sanding block and 7/0 paper you will notice low spots building up and high spots reducing. Repeat the procedure until you ultimately see a level surface. Keep the sandpaper clean with a stiff brush and also by flicking a finger against the block to shake out loose dust and abrasive. When satisfied with the varnish surface set the panel aside for three or four days to let the varnish dry thoroughly.

Polishing. This next step in the finishing process makes the difference between an ordinary finish and a professional finish. Polishing can give your varnished surface a satin sheen or a high gloss whichever you prefer. For a satin finish use 360 or 400 wet-or-dry silicon carbide paper dipped in a pan of water and wrapped around a sanding block. Lightly sand all surfaces. Next rub with pumice powder. Take a piece of heavy old cloth such as cloth towel. Wet the cloth and dip into a small mound of pumice. Rub all surfaces. If you want a higher sheen repeat the rubbing operation with rottenstone powder instead of pumice. Now if you prefer a glossier sheen repeat with rubbing oil and rottenstone. Oil as a rubbing vehicle is slower than water and makes a shinier surface than water. The choice is yours.

In place of pumice and rottenstone a prepared paste of rubbing powders and cutting oil, called rubbing compound, is sometimes preferred. It cuts faster, is simpler to handle and produces a high mirror-like polish. After the rubbing operation remove residue with cheesecloth and complete the clean-up with good furniture polish such as OZ cream polish which cleans as it polishes.

French polish. The name is well known, but the process of French polishing is a mystery to many hobby woodworkers; yet the art of French polishing is several centuries old. Briefly, it consists of shellac applications built up in layers with a rubbing pad, not a brush. It is one of the most beautiful finishes, but it takes practice to do well.

Most of those who do French polishing have their own special methods. The basic method given here will enable newcomers to experiment, preferably on scrap veneers before attempting to finish valued marquetry.

The rubbing pad, which pros call the rubber, is cloth. Wadded up it should be at least the size of a ping pong ball, larger for areas larger than the average marquetry picture. A lint-free cloth, soft old linen for example, is used for the outside of the pad. The inside is packed with cotton waste and should be quite compact.

Mix one part of fresh white shellac with two parts alcohol. Dip the pad into the shellac mixture and squeeze out the liquid. Sprinkle a few drops of linseed oil on the pad as a lubricant. Tap the pad on a piece of clean brown paper to equalize distribution. This is an important part of the process. Never use too much mixture on the pad. If you apply too much the coat will build too fast and develop streaks. The pad should be wet enough to glide over the surface and dry enough to avoid rapid build-up. Apply in a linear pattern. Overlap each stroke about 1/2" with a gentle, smooth motion that should never stop abruptly. Make repeat applications with the same pad and materials as many times as necessary to achieve good coverage and a durable surface.

Now make another pad in the same way. Dampen it lightly with alcohol. Sprinkle the veneer surface sparsely with 4/0 pumice powder. Work the pad over the surface in a circular or figure 8 motion using gentle pressure. Repeat this application until pores of the wood are filled. Pumice must be in the pores, not on the surface.

For a final polishing use lemon oil as a lubricant. Dip your finger in lemon oil and dab the oil on the surface at several spots. Use the original rubbing pad to distribute. Gently rub over the surface in a circular direction. If streaks appear rub over the area with a clean cloth dampened with alcohol.

A beautiful French polish finish calls for patience and practice. There are variations of technique among skilled polishers. Orange shellac instead of white can be used. The proportion of shellac to alcohol is variable. Pad materials can be experimented with, and the type of lubricating oil can be determined best by trial.

Other finishing materials and techniques are suited to marquetry. The foregoing methods for clear finish, without stains or coloring agents, simply indicate the recommended approach to finishing your marquetry pictures in ways that richly enhance the colors and figures of veneers.

13. Fragmentation. Metal, bone and other inlays

Veneer cannot easily depict breaking waves. Sometimes in the hands of the inexperienced waves look like wood. Veneer has a hard time looking like a gorgeously colored red and yellow maple tree in autumn. Realism is not easy to create with veneers. When badly done realism in the extreme can downgrade a picture. Done well of course, as in many examples in this book, it is admirable.

There is a special technique beginners and pros alike can follow in making things look realistic. If used sparingly in a picture it makes remarkably good ocean waves, colorful autumn trees, stone walls, shrubbery and other multi-colored objects. The technique is called fragmentation. It utilizes colored veneers. They are cut into tiny fragments and packed with glue into a predetermined shape. The form for shaping this mass of veneer fragments and glue is a window cut in the piece of veneer being used as background in a picture.

Cutting very small squares of chosen veneer and arranging them this way and that according to color effect desired seems to be the best way to imitate autumn foliage. (13-1) The same tiny squares arranged in more formal patterns make a mosaic pattern like the Scotties. (13-2) A mixture of squares, diamonds and bits and pieces can be worked into a patterned subject like the owl. (13-3) Breaking waves are made up of longer strips and splinters. Even shavings cut from the edge of scrap veneers are useful in fragmentation. Imitating grass is one use.

To develop a fragmented object in a veneer picture choose several pieces of

13-1. Realistic tree composed of tiny fragments packed solid with white glue in shaped window

veneer of different but appropriate color. The edge of the forest in autumn, for example, made use of red, green, yellow, brown and black veneers. To experiment with the technique cut a few pieces of each veneer color into manageable strips or squares. Put clear tape on front and back to prevent split-

107

13-2. Veneer squares laid in formal mosaic-like patterns show another fragmentation technique

13-3. Fragmented owl demonstrates skillful control in assembling small fragments of veneer

ting and splintering while you are cutting into thin strips. Develop a practical but simple means of cutting veneers into long strips of uniform width. (13-4)

Use your craft knife to help you peel the clear tape off the cut strips. You may break a few. Have some replacements on hand. Now cut the strips into tiny squares about the width of veneer thickness. Cut with craft knife or single-edge razor blade. (13-5) This cutting operation is a little more like chopping than actually cutting. Just pressure the cutting tool through the veneer. Have a few plastic pill bottles or parts boxes ready to store the cut pieces. Keep colors separate for the present.

Autumn trees. The edge of the forest enclosing the corn field needs a lot of little fragments, but when you have cut enough veneer in different colors to form just two trees, one at each end of the forest, you should start making the tree at the right. As with other marquetry methods you first cut a tree-shape window in chosen background veneer. Working with one tree at a time you have the opportunity to frame the tree with black or dark brown fragments to form a shadow outline. Without shadow the trees would not look like trees, but more like a multi-colored fence or some such thing. Now you will appreciate the earlier instruction to keep fragments separated by color.

You are going to fill the window with fragments, working from the back of the background veneer. Turn the veneer over for a moment while you lay veneer tape on the front side of background veneer to cover and seal off the window so that no fragments can fall through. It's a good idea to cut a second window, this one at the opposite end of the forest, and cover it with tape on the face side. With two cutout windows, far separated, you will be able to work on the second window without waiting for the first to dry.

Turn the background over again to work from the back. Sprinkle a bit of dark veneer against each side edge of the window to create shadow. Now sprinkle one or two chosen colors next to the shadow. Keep filling window opening. Push and shift little

13-4. Two veneer scraps held against stop board control width of thin veneer strips being cut

13-5. Cutting strips into tiny squares. Hold a few under thumb. Thumbnail acts as knife guide

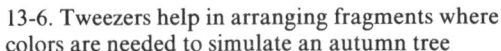

13-6. Tweezers help in arranging fragments where colors are needed to simulate an autumn tree

13-7. Tree-shaped window in background veneer is filled tight with fragments, packed with glue

fragments around with tweezers to create a multi-colored autumn tree. (13-6) Build the fragments above the surface of background. This is the back of the picture and later will be sanded flat as necessary.

Squeeze white glue over the mass of fragments. Wait a couple of minutes to allow the glue to tack. Then use a spatula or a flexible steel rule to press glue into the mass. (13-7) Waiting for tack allows the mass to solidify somewhat. Don't stir the pieces around and destroy your color arrangement. As tack continues to develop press harder to form a compact mass and to fill the window tightly. Add

109

13-8. Colorful autumn trees are formed one at a time of veneer fragments packed in background

fragments as necessary to mound above the background veneer. Be sure to pack fragments firmly around the window edges.

Fill the window at the other end of the forest and then wait long enough for both windows to harden thoroughly. Continue with the same method, working on two separated trees at a session. For guidance in arranging colors try to locate in advance a pleasing color picture of a forest in autumn. After the completed tree line has dried under weights for a day or two you can level the back with sandpaper. Hold the assembly up to a light source and inspect for cracks and tiny holes. Fill from the back. For this purpose make a mix of veneer sawdust and white glue. Allow patches to dry, then sand again. After mounting the completed marquetry picture on a panel apply several coats of clear varnish. Polyurethane varnish is especially good in accentuating the lively colors used for the fragmented forest. (13-8)

Fragmented shading. Often veneer pictures contain elements that could contribute more reality if they blended into their neighbors. The technique of fragmentation can be used to accomplish blending and shading. By experiment you will be able to work out the technical requirements of shading. The principle to work on is to make smaller and smaller fragments. The smaller you use, the more subtle is the shading. With practice you will invent some tricks of combining colors so skillfully that dark areas of shadow will turn lighter and lighter so gradually as to imitate an artist's brush.

Windows and doors. Tiny elements in a picture are sometimes made with a single piece of veneer. Windows and doors are often made in that way. Irregular small shapes are even harder to make than small windows. Some of these elements would look better if they had more textural character than conveyed by a one-color piece. Fragmentation could be the best solution. It certainly would be easier than fitting irregular shapes and tiny squares. For some of these tiny elements very small fragments, virtually bits of shavings and even a mix of sawdust from colored veneers, can be packed into the openings and secured with white glue.

Many other opportunities are waiting for a practical technique such as fragmentation. Experimentation with this method could solve some special problems which to now have not easily been overcome with standard techniques.

Techniques for inlaying metals and other materials in veneer

Materials other than veneer are sometimes incorporated in marquetry work—metal, ivory or bone, tortoise shell, and mother-of-pearl which comes from the inner layer of certain sea shells. These materials are much harder to work than veneer. For this reason they usually are cut to shape and then inserted in openings made in the veneer assembly. If the assembly has already been mounted on a solid panel a recess must be cut to receive the pre-cut inlay. Some craftworkers prefer the recess method even though it requires special equipment. The recessing method is called inlay. Inserting the new material into a veneer assembly could be called inlay or marquetry whichever you prefer. There is a third option. Some soft metals may be treated as veneer and cut simultaneously with the background veneer. This method was demonstrated in chapters on saw-cutting. The expense and scarcity of ivory, tortoise shell and mother-of-pearl limit their use. Most inlay work today makes use of metals such as soft brass, aluminum and copper.

Metal chosen for inlaying must be at least as thick as the veneer into which it will be inlaid. And it should be soft. Brass is most often preferred. Determine softness by bending a small tip of one corner of the sheet. If it springs back to original shape it is too hard and must be annealed. This can be done by marking a few areas of one surface with a bar of soap. Hold the sheet of metal, soap side up, with a pair of tongs. Lower it over a gas flame until the soap markings sizzle and bubble. Allow the metal to cool in the air. Do not quench in water.

If you are going to inlay shaped brass designs cut off a square the required size from the annealed brass sheet. Trace or paste a pattern on the metal and cut to shape with a fret saw or power scroll saw. If you want to inlay brass strips you can purchase small brass bars of various thicknesses, widths and lengths. The problem is finding a source for exactly your requirements. You may end up cutting your own strips from a brass sheet. Use a marking gauge to mark off the required width of strip to be cut. First, however, make certain the guiding edge of the sheet is perfectly straight. A good precaution with any sheet is to file the edge with a mill file. Hold the file level and work the entire length from end to end without filing across the edge. Cut off the strips with a hack saw and file down to required width. The ideal thickness of inlay metal is 3/32". When inlaid in veneer this thickness leaves about 1/32" above the wood surface. It will be filed level when you are preparing your veneer assembly for finishing after mounting.

Inlaying mounted assemblies. To inlay in a solid surface such as a mounted marquetry picture or a veneered box lid, tray or other solid surface you will need equipment for cutting a recess. A tool called a hand router plane can be used for straight recesses or for cleaning out a recess which has been started with a knife. An inlay cutter looking somewhat like a marking gauge can make straight or circular cuts. An electric router is the most versatile of all. It can rout a recess of just about any shape you need.

To start a recess for metal—the most popular material other than veneer—mark the mounted veneer surface to show the precise outline of the inlay. Use a very fine pencil or a craft knife for marking.

To accommodate a hand router plane to your work you may have to grind the cutter to smaller width, especially if thin strips are to be laid. For straight recesses you can work out a guide or fence by clamping a straight strip of wood across the area for the router plane to ride against. Take very shallow cuts, increasing cutter depth as you progress. For final cuts be sure to adjust the blade to make cuts no deeper than your inlay. Actually the depth of recess should be somewhat less than the inlay to allow for filing flush at a later time. Exercise extreme care in using any router or grooving tool. They are especially hazardous tools and can readily damage your work or injure your hands. Practice on scrap wood before starting on your valuable marquetry project.

Electric router. These machines require indoctrination. Study instructions in books or manufacturer's pamphlets before using the tool. The electric router removes material fast and efficiently. Select a router bit of proper shape and size for your inlay. Set the cutting depth so that just a bit of top edge of inlay will stand above the surface for filing flush. Ordinarily it is best to choose a smaller width of cutter bit than the required recess. Enlarging a recess is easy. The electric router leaves rounded ends at corners. Use a small chisel to square the corner.

Straight strips of metal being prepared for inlaying should have ends mitered. This is accomplished by cutting off the piece at 45 degrees and using a mill file to true up the angle. Lay this strip in the recess. Push the mitered end fully into the corner and mark the other end for length. Allow extra for filing a miter on that end. Replace the strip in the groove. Do not force inlay strips into position. They have to be removed. Repeat the mitering and fitting until all strips fit snugly where they belong. Remove after fitting. Number each strip.

Clean out the routed grooves with a small brush. Remove all sawdust and metal filings. Lightly coat the grooves with white or yellow glue. Remove burrs from metal strips and rub the bottom of the metal with vinegar or clove of garlic or onion to remove all traces of grease. This trick also cleans the brass and improves its bond with glue. Now press the strips tightly into respective grooves. Tap lightly with a hammer. When the inlay is satisfactory clamp the entire piece between cauls or place under weights for overnight.

When the assembly comes out of clamps it is ready for surfacing. Use a large, flat, fine-cut file to cut down the projecting metal. Exercise utmost care to avoid file marks on veneer. Brush off filings after each stroke so none can be ground into the wood. After filing use your sharp cabinet scraper to continue the surfacing. Again remove all metal scrapings after each pass with the scraper. For final surfacing use 220 wet-or-dry paper and follow with 500. Brass will be beautiful under any clear finish of your choice.

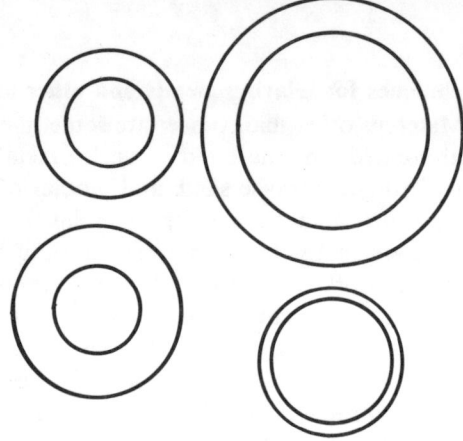

13-9. Rings cut from metal tubing or washers can be used as inlay parts in marquetry assemblies

Many interesting designs can be worked out with metal tubing. Useful shapes and sizes are almost unlimited. (13-9) Use a hack saw to slice off a metal ring of necessary thickness. Square and straighten the edges with a file. Lay the ring in position on the veneer and trace its shape inside and outside. Rout or cut a recess if inlaying into a solid background. Cut an opening with knife or saw if inlaying into a sheet of veneer. (13-10) Inlay with glue and file down the projection.

13-10. Hand router cuts recess in panel to take metal ring and veneer circle inset with initial

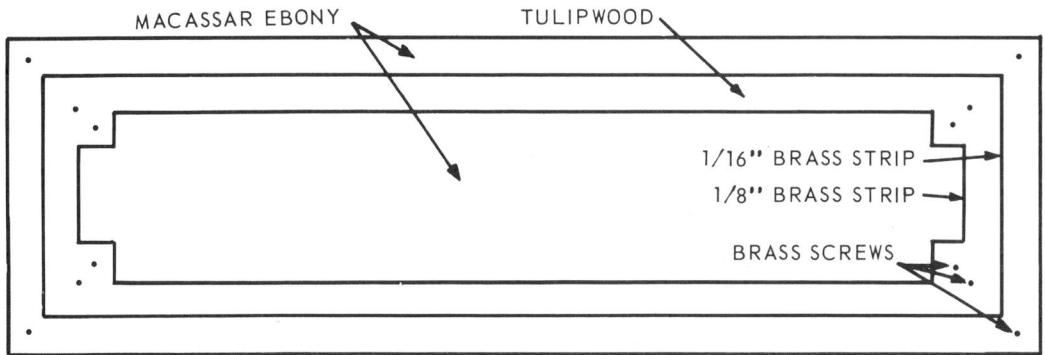

MACASSAR EBONY   TULIPWOOD

1/16" BRASS STRIP
1/8" BRASS STRIP
BRASS SCREWS

13-11. Panel for box top or tray combines veneer with inlaid brass strips and screws, heads cut

Follow work instructions given for metal strips. Metal rod can supply solid discs for inlaying. Brass screws can be driven into a mounted veneer surface. Heads should then be snipped off and screws filed to form a flush surface with the wood. (13-11)

Designs of irregular shape can be cut first and then inlaid in recesses routed in already mounted veneers. This is delicate work. Exercise extreme care to avoid any mistake that will damage a fine marquetry assembly. In fact, you will be able to avoid the risk by deciding in advance on the inlay work while the veneer face is still an unmounted assembly. This simpler method is the same system that was used in earlier chapters for fretsaw and scroll-saw marquetry.

Paste your inlay pattern in position on the veneer assembly. Prepare an oversize piece of metal of the same thickness as the veneer. Tape the metal on the back of the veneer under the pattern area. Use a pin vise with a No. 60 drill to make a saw hole through veneer and metal at some point on the pattern outline where there is an intersecting point of design. Use your fingers to twist the drill which is being held in the pin vise. Through the hole just made, now insert a 4/0 jeweler's blade and fasten it in the saw you are going to cut with. Hold the work on a tilted table and follow the simultaneous bevel-cutting technique (13-12) which makes the tightest possible joint between veneer and metal inlay. After cutting has been done insert the metal inlay into the window opening in the veneer. The aluminum helmet in

the crest illustrated in Chapter 2 was made in this way. Before mounting, when you are roughly sanding the back surface to be glued, degrease the piece of metal and use rough sandpaper on the metal surface for better glue bonding.

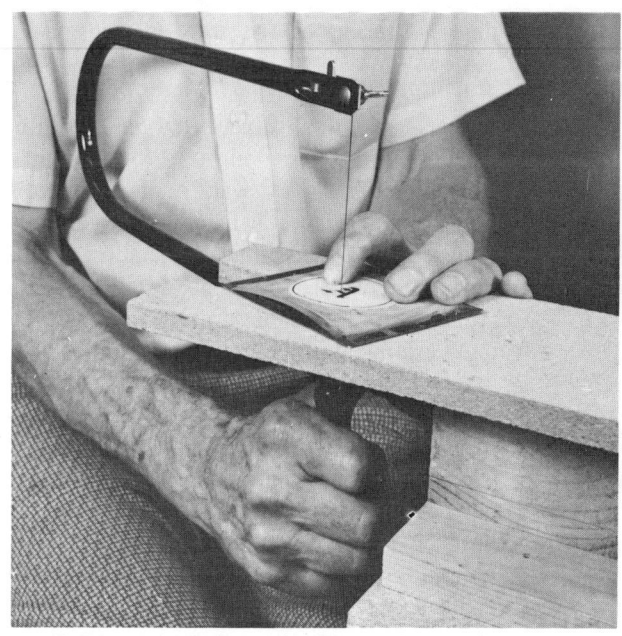

13-12. Metal taped beneath background veneer is cut simultaneously. Bevel-cutting technique

113

14. Sand shading—the third dimension in marquetry

It would be difficult to find a picture subject in marquetry that could not benefit by at least a touch or two of shading. Portraits, birds, animals, country roads, city skylines, forests, fields and harbors all gain a degree of reality when some of their elements are vignetted with soft shading.

Brush painting on veneers is considered to be a sacrilege by all who revere the natural beauty of wood. But shading created by dipping veneer parts in hot sand for a quick and mild scorching is universally accepted. Sand shading of veneer parts can blend, shade, fade, reduce or increase contrast. The trick is to make the shading subtle and to use it sparingly. No other rules can be advanced because shading is wholly an artistic decision—where to add it to create the illusion of depth. Shading is the third dimension in marquetry.

It is not likely that your stockpile of veneers can furnish a piece that has the natural gradation of tone you need for a particular effect. You may want a dark shadow being cast across water from a boat riding at anchor. Of course you need a shadow that is dark at the waterline and grows light until it vignettes and disappears in water. Or you need soft facial shadows in a portrait, or delicate shading on petals of a flower to separate petals of the same kind of veneer. Every picture has a place or two for shading.

Sand shading usually is done right on the cut part. Other methods of shading can be used on areas of a completed picture after mounting. Sand shading on cut parts is more controllable and less risky. If you over-scorch a cut piece you can replace it without damage to the entire picture.

Equipment for sand shading is easy to assemble. A frying pan or similar metal dish is needed to contain the sand. An old tablespoon, long tweezers or tongs, a source of heat, either gas or electric. The best sand for the purpose is clean, sharp sand obtainable at a pet shop. If you choose to use beach sand strain it and then bag it in burlap or other loosely woven cloth for washing. Even so, it won't be as clean as you can buy.

Pour sand in the pan to a depth of about 1 1/2". Put the pan over a heat source. Turn to medium heat. Leave for 20 to 30 minutes. Do not plunge the cut piece of veneer in hot sand until you have tested one or two scrap pieces of the same kind of veneer. Shading will start and be darkest at the immersed edge. It will fade at the upper edge of the sand. Hold veneer with tweezers. Immerse one edge into the hot sand. (14-1) Do not allow veneer to touch the bottom of the pan. Slowly count 101, 102, 103, 104, 105. That's about five seconds. Withdraw the veneer and examine the area that was in the sand. See if the lower edge has darkened and if this tone gradually lightens higher on the piece. (14-2) If not right try slightly hotter sand. If still not dark enough try another count to 105. Experience has shown that five seconds is about the right timing. It is better to increase heat than to increase time. This procedure is charring the veneer. Do not over-scorch or you will make the veneer very brittle. When satisfied with the shading lightly sand the veneer, then moisten it slightly and place under weights for awhile before you inset it into your marquetry assembly.

There are a few variables to work out for each different veneer you work with. Heat

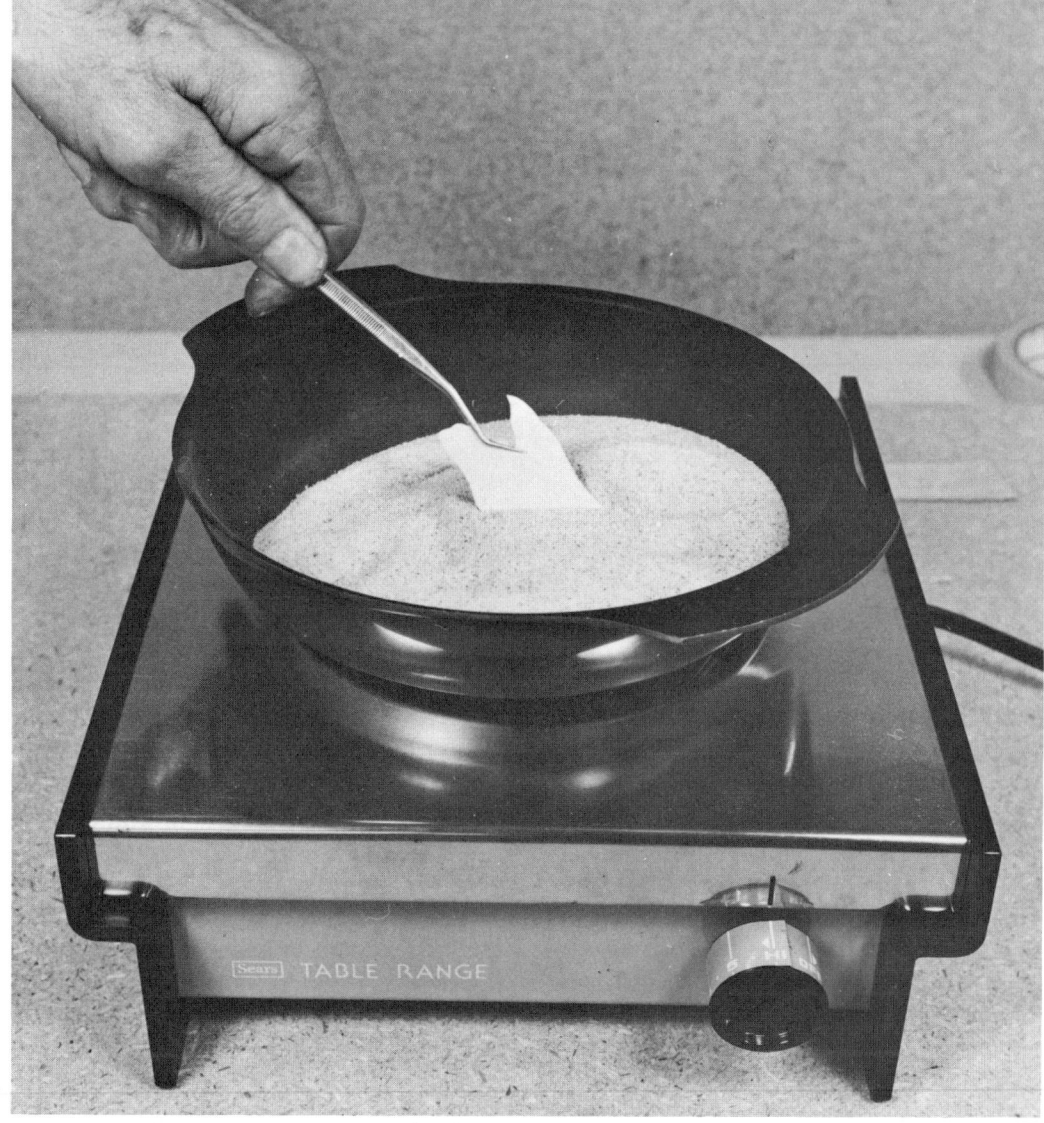

14-1. Usually shading is done before the cut part of veneer is assembled. Immerse edge in hot sand

and timing are important. Other factors are the mounding of sand and the way you hold the veneer part in the sand. If the piece is to be shaded evenly insert it into sand horizontally. This position gives the best overall even shading. If you require shading only along the edge immerse just the edge. For the softest shading, mound up the sand to move it away from the heat. Immerse into the mound and allow somewhat longer treatment. Contoured edges can be shaded just around the perimeter of the piece by either mounding or scooping sand to form a convex or concave contour.

You may want to shade only the center area of a cut part. Instead of dipping veneer into sand, use your spoon to pour hot sand where you want shading. First, tape scrap veneer over areas you do not want shaded. This method of masking obviously leaves an open area. Hold the masked veneer part at a slight angle over the sand pit. Spoon hot sand from the bottom of the pan over the open area of veneer. Allow sand to fall back into the pan. Repeat this spooning operation until the desired shade is reached. Be sure that you are shading the side of veneer that is to be the face side in the picture. You may be able to skip the masking trick and carefully spoon hot sand on one or more areas. Let

14-2. After five seconds in hot sand lift veneer out to inspect shading. Increase time or heat

your requirements dictate the best method.

When just a spot or two is to be shaded you may want to try the pebble shading method instead of using hot sand. A collection of various sizes of pebbles is all you need. Heat the pebbles as you heated sand. Use tweezers to pick up and place individual pebbles on veneer. Work only one spot at a time so each spot can be monitored and scorching can be avoided. Pebble shading has been quite successful in shading foliage. Many novel effects have been achieved by pebble shading in localized spots and in scattered areas as well.

Regardless of your method of shading with hot sand or pebbles the heat is going to dry out the veneer and cause slight shrinkage. To overcome this problem be sure to moisten the veneer with a sponge immediately after shading and place under weights.

Experiment on identical veneer scraps. Be patient and try variations of all factors. Be sure to brush away all sand from shaded pieces. One grain of remaining sand can cause havoc to finishing coats.

Shading without sand. A recent innovation for shading veneers uses a piece of 1/4" aluminum 8 x 8. This metal plate is laid over a gas burner and heated by moderate heat.

The cut part of veneer is held with tweezers so that the edge to be shaded can be brought close to the heat source. Usually 1/16 to 1/8 is close enough to accomplish the desired degree of shading. Care must be taken to keep the veneer from making even momentary contact with the hot metal plate, or the veneer will be charred beyond use. One big advantage of using a plate as large as 8 x 8 is that there is a temperature drop-off from the center toward the edges.

For shading contours of very finely pointed details a pencil type of soldering iron with interchangeable tips is useful. The operation is slow but it offers good control. Another advantage is in seeing just how much shading you are getting. A pyrographic pen used for wood-burning also gives visual inspection as you apply heat. Most pens have an adjustment for heat. When you use this type of instrument or a soldering iron you can do localized shading on a mounted picture prior to finishing. Allow the heated points time to accomplish shading without applying pressure or you will dent the veneer and make finishing more difficult. Move the instrument slowly over the area somewhat as an artist applies light coloring with a brush.

116

15. Birds in marquetry—selecting and cutting veneer

The inclusion of birds in marquetry seems to be uncommon; yet there are not many subjects more thoroughly adaptable to the medium. Beginners and experienced alike can apply their own level of skill to cutting veneers to simulate birds. The results can be amazingly realistic.

Think in marquetry terms when you study a close-up photograph of a bird. Notice that its formations fit the same scheme as other marquetry subjects; that is, the feathers can be composed of small pieces. An assembly of small pieces can provide shape, color and shading. Generally you will reproduce large feathers one by one and give the impression

of small feathers by running wood grain in the right direction. Examination shows that feathers are made of strong, straight lines that rarely change direction within an individual piece. The straight parallel grain of wood exactly imitates the parallel barbs arising from the central shaft of a feather.

If we omit brightly colored birds from consideration we can find natural veneers in reds, browns, tans, grays and whites which can faithfully reproduce the coloring of many earth colored birds such as owls, eagles, partridges, grouse, hawks, mockingbirds and many others. Even a bird's outline adapts itself to marquetry. Look at a

15-1. Detail from marquetry bird and the pattern it developed from shows how arrows and shading are included on full-size pattern to serve as guide to selecting, cutting and placing veneer

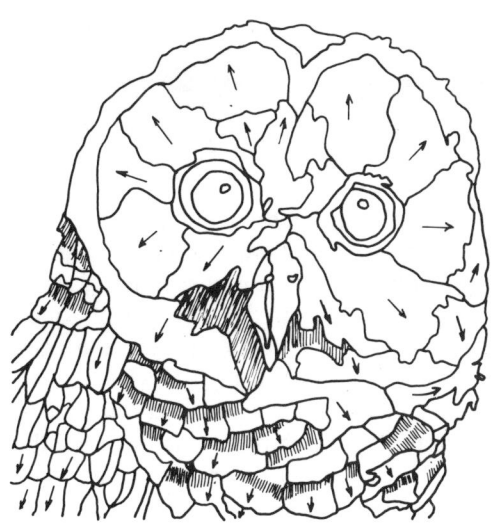

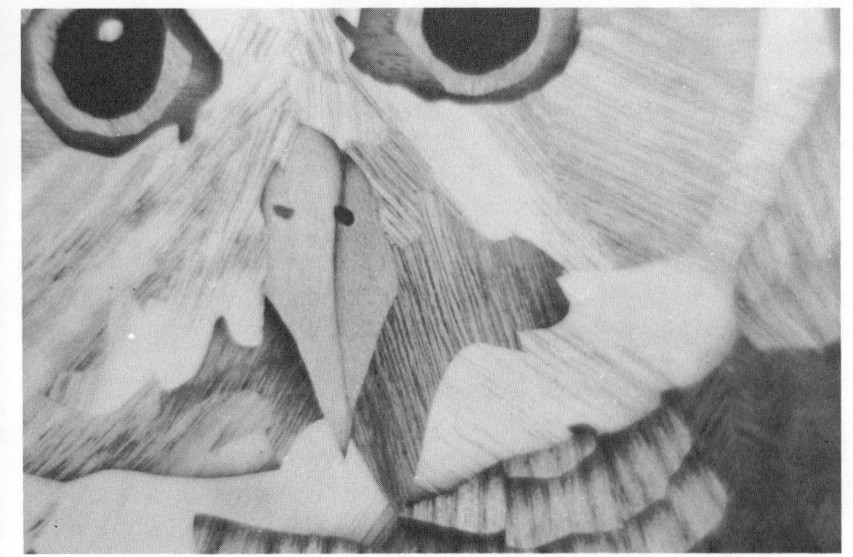

15-2. Olive ash with strong grain made facial feathers in this bird. Striped olive ash used for breast feathers. The two blend very well. A white section of the same veneer made ring of light feathers at periphery of face. Beak shadow made of olive ash sand shaded to darken it

15-3. Eyes are focal point in birds. Highlights are critical in establishing intention and mood of the bird. Highlights are triangular darts of light veneer set in dark veneer pupil. Round highlights are non-aggressive while triangular darts suggest curious or predatory attitude

bird's silhouette and notice the multitude of points. Individual feathers are pointed, as are wing tips, tail feathers and beak. Points are one of the easiest shapes to accomplish with any cutting tool used in marquetry—craft knife, fret saw and power scroll saw.

For source material study photographs in magazines and books. Photographs usually are heavy on shadow contrast. When interpreted in marquetry these shadows form

the basis of a strong three dimensional effect which greatly enhances realism. Photographs, however, do not always tell a story. Nature drawings on the other hand often capture dramatic activity—an eagle diving, an osprey soaring, a nighthawk in swift pursuit. The bird in action may appeal to you more than the bird at rest, but even the bird on a tree limb or atop a fence post can be depicted preparing for action. Birds at rest can be imbued with mood. An owl sitting quietly against a dark sky suggests a somber mood with a suggestion of the owl's potential as a night hunter.

Tempting as it may at first appear, a brightly colored bird does not come through marquetry with the textural quality of a bird made with natural colored woods. Dyed veneers impart more brilliance, but those dyed veneers you would be working with lack the necessary figuration and grain necessary for good feather reproduction. Furthermore, sand shading cannot produce a realistic shadow effect on dyed wood. Blue dyed wood scorches to brown. Red comes brown. It isn't natural shading. But on woods already naturally brown or tan the subtle brown shading is visually pleasant. And shading is critical to a realistic reproduction.

Preparing the pattern. The earlier chapter on designs and patterns should be studied further if you are in doubt about pattern requirements for marquetry. There are optional ways for making patterns. The projection method has a special advantage with bird patterns. The size and direction of the subject is so easily adjusted when using a photo slide in a projector. If a second bird of the same species, for example, is to be incorporated in the scene, a smaller image of the same slide can be cast on your drawing paper almost instantly. Also, when working with bird subjects light and dark areas become very important and can be seen more clearly by the projection method than by various tracing techniques.

Follow the usual system for pattern making by drawing a general outline of the entire bird in pencil. Fill in basic background details if appropriate. Outline the eyes with particular care. Be very detailed. Note the eye highlight if present. If you have any doubt about how well you have drawn the eye, erase the work and start it again. This is the most important single feature. Step back and try to visualize light and dark areas of the body. They are there even though they may call for some imagination to bring out. Some light and dark areas run across feather details. This is acceptable because it in-

dicates shadows which are essential to a three dimensional effect. Trace in these areas in full detail even where they do not make much sense. When the project is complete they will provide realism. Indicate by pencil shading the dark areas. Use arrows in each area to show feather direction. (15-1) Small feathers of head, neck and breast unless very close are best handled as areas rather than as individual feathers. Larger body feathers such as primaries, secondaries and tail should be outlined individually. The central shaft should be drawn in and the direction of feather barbs as they run V-shaped from the shaft shown by arrows. Within reason make the pattern detailed. It is easier to delete than add when the pattern is complete.

The basic veneer. A bird usually is planned around one major veneer called the basic veneer. An ideal basic veneer should have strong grain, both light and dark areas, and a curving figure. Veneers having both light and dark sections are better for bright and shadowed areas, supplemented by sand shading, than a second darker wood even though the grain pattern of the second wood is similar. The second veneer invariably blends poorly and cannot reproduce a smooth gradual shading of feathers. It is better to stay with the same basic veneer for shadow effect and to change wood only when the feather color changes. Prominent grain reproduces feather structure best. The ideal veneer should have strong figure slightly curving. Curving figure is useful in the head where feather direction curves outward like a pinwheel and is important for wingtips as well as curved surfaces of breast and shoulders. Failure to use curving figure in these areas often produces a stiff, unnatural appearance.

Two veneers which are very close to an ideal basic veneer for bird marquetry are figured English walnut and olive ash, figured and striped varieties. A peculiarity of walnut is that sanding causes the grain to disappear; however, the grain comes back again when the wood is finished. Olive ash has large areas of nearly white wood. This is excellent for white birds because its grain texture is stronger than other white woods such as holly and sycamore. Olive ash develops hints of brown streaking suggesting shadow detail when it is finished. Striped olive ash blends well with the figured variety in color and is also useful in areas where anatomic detail in feather structure is not required. (15-2)

Color harmony. Most natural woods have either yellow or red overtones. Even white woods follow this pattern. With few exceptions a mix of red and yellow gives an unpleasant effect. Be aware of this factor when selecting secondary veneers. English walnut tends toward red, while olive ash tends toward yellow.

Even though no veneer is completely white, especially after the yellowing effects of finish and the passage of time, white birds are good subjects. The secret is in the contrast between subject and background. Even a slightly yellow holly or olive ash appears white when placed against darker veneers. The darker the background the greater the illusion of white.

Background can create the mood of the scene. Figured avodire simulates a brilliant sky. The dark shadows of walnut burl establish a sinister or lonely mood. A woodland background of goncalo alves gives a mysterious midnight effect. The swirl of crotch aspen or walnut gives a feeling that something unknown lies just outside the picture. Well-joined walnut can give the appearance of soft fur. Daniellia alters its light and dark areas as the viewer changes his angle of view.

Working procedure. Landscape subjects usually start with large pieces of veneer into which smaller pieces are cut and inset. This technique is not recommended for birds. Feather direction is constantly changing, and no single large piece of veneer can duplicate it. Instead a jigsaw puzzle approach is best, making and fitting small pieces. Start at the head. Cut each small piece separately in the correct feather direction. If the area on the pattern is too large to allow proper grain change, make two pieces for that area, each in a slightly different orientation. Cutting should start at a central point and work toward the outer border.

The bird's head is usually the focal point of the picture. The viewer's attention is first drawn to the head. Although the body, wings and tail give the illusion of motion, texture, color and bulk, it is the head that sets the tone of attack, defense, watchfulness, stillness or whatever is intended. It therefore is important to work and re-work the head until it is as realistic as you can possibly make it. The focal point of the head is the eye, and the most critical detail in the eye is the highlight. Despite its small size the highlight gives a bird its lifelike appearance. Without a highlight animation is almost impossible. When you make the pattern be sure to draw an accurate highlight. If not present in your original source picture add it.

Highlight in the eye. All avian eyes are divided into a round black central spot called the pupil and a larger colored outer portion called the iris. Highlights appear within the darkness of the pupil. There are exceptions, so follow your model carefully. The shape of the highlight, small as it may be, clearly sets the intent of the bird. Most highlights are triangular with their base resting on the outer rim of the pupil and the pointed end directed toward the center. The taller and more pointed the triangle the more aggressive the bird appears. An attacking bird has a sharp triangle, a curious foraging bird a wider triangle. One or more oval or irregular circular highlights in an eye imply peacefulness as in a bird at rest or perhaps a baby. (15-2 and 15-3)

Highlights are quite small. To make a highlight, start by using soft-cutting dark wood for the pupil. Ebony is right for color, but hard to cut without splitting. Walnut burl is a good choice. Cut in the triangular highlight. Cutting a tiny triangle with a knife is quite easy if you break the usual rule of cutting from the back. Select a piece of sycamore or holly that has been cut into and is left with a few shaped points. Find a point of the right size for your triangle. Hold it in place over the triangular window in the pupil. Cut off the point and press it into the window. Rub glue on the back and sand the front to level the inset highlight.

15-4. Feathers are represented by different techniques. Type I method was followed for feathers at right. Made in two pieces with grain forming V pattern. At left feathers are Type II, each cut in one piece from prominently grained veneer. Shadows created by sand shading add depth and give realistic appearance

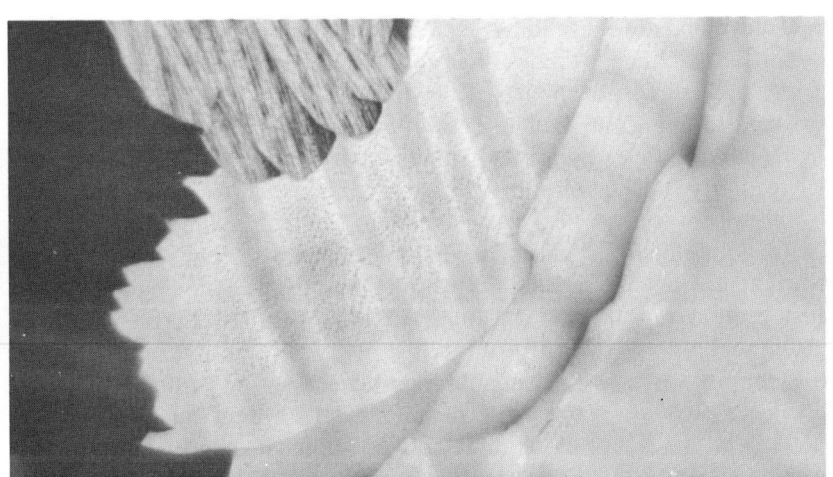

15-5. Feathers at bottom right of this detail depict Type III method which simulates a lot of small feathers by larger pieces of veneer. Moiree willow used to carry on same feather direction as olive ash. Irregular joints avoid straight lines which are uncommon in living subjects

Feather technique. In marquetry feathers fall into one of three categories. Type I consists of a prominent shaft with barbs coming off in a V pattern. Type II is for smaller breast and back feathers. Though visible they are small and tend to run together. Type III is for down-like feathers which appear as a soft texture only on the belly, legs and head. Some individual ones are visible. Usually the wing-tip primaries would be done by the Type I method. Method, however, is dependent upon the size that the feather appears to be in the project. As distance from the viewer increases, feather size diminishes. The wing-tip primaries may then be more suitably done by Type II method. (15-6)

Type I technique. Cut each feather in two parts. Grain is used to show barbs arising from the shaft in a V pattern. The joint line gives the appearance of the shaft. (15-4)

Type II. For feathers in this class run grain in the same direction as the feather shaft. Either striped or figured veneer is suitable. Cut each feather separately, but vary the direction of grain each time according to the direction lines on the pattern. (15-4)

15-6. Feathers at a distance call for a mix of construction techniques. The rules change. Large wing-tip feathers now are better with Type II method, and small wing feathers look more realistic with Type III method

Type III. In this class, feathers are to be cut in one piece. Individual feathers are largely ignored. Most important is that the grain in these areas runs in the right direction. As feathers of this type tend to curve, choose veneer with a noticeable curving figure. The joints are best cut irregularly so as to hide the linear lines that otherwise would occur. Proper blending, with joint lines minimized, is the key to realism here. For an almost iridescent effect when using yellow woods try figured moiree willow. This veneer has pronounced mottle running at a right angle to grain, producing a striking silky effect. (15-5)

A bird with a spotted breast poses a problem. No wood figure contains dark spots. Either ignore the spotting or try a piece of zebrano. This is yellowish with pronounced dark stripes, thin in width. If using zebrano cut the breast into many small pieces. Be careful never to match up the dark lines. Disruption of lines gives the appearance of a spotted surface.

If the feet are light in color, regardless of what color they are supposed to be, use figured harewood. Often the figure in certain sections of harewood is small and irregular much like the scaly texture of a bird's legs. If the legs in your model are darker use a dark area of walnut burl as if they are in shadow.

Sand shading bird subjects. Proper use of shading techniques is critical for a good three dimensional effect. In a bird assembly about seventy-five percent of all pieces are shaded before being glued in place. Extensive shading is based upon the fact that in strong light each feather, as it overlaps the next, casts its shadow on the proximal end of the underlying one. Failure to shade, leaves a flat and bland look to the project. Feathers will run into each other in a way that is not at all true to life.

Using a darker veneer is a poor substitute for sand shading. The edge of a shadow should fade gradually into surrounding area. Sand shading mimics this effect; whereas a change of veneer causes an abrupt border. Also with sand shading the shadow area retains the same color and texture as the lighter area. To realize the importance of sand shading consider the problem of a shadow cast on feathers by another object such as beak or tree branch. It is far better to shade the entire shadow than to substitute another veneer. The superiority of sand shading the basic veneer is evident for all situations except perhaps for a really strong shadow. (15-2)

Sand shading for bird subjects should be done after the piece has been cut to shape. Equipment and techniques are covered in a special chapter on sand shading. A few further tips for feather shading may be helpful. If a dark, shallow and well-defined burn is required take a spoon, thin the depth of sand and burn close to the pan surface. If a lighter, deeper and softly graduated burn is needed pile the hot sand deeply at the center. Take advantage of the curved top of the mound to burn a concave shadow evenly. Hold very small pieces in a spoon and press the spoon into hot sand. Sand shading drives moisture from the wood. To avoid consequent shrinkage place the pieces immediately between moist towels.

Moisture replacement works best on small pieces and then only when the burn has not been excessive. When shrinkage occurs in large pieces you might try laying them on the pattern and then compensating by making the adjoining piece a little larger to fill the gap. The alternative is to remake the first piece. It is good practice to lay the large piece first and fill around it with smaller adjoining pieces, making the smaller pieces a bit oversize to fill out.

Bird assembly and background. From methods followed up to this point it should be clear that the bird is often constructed outside its ultimate background. Few background woods could tolerate the alternate system of cutting background windows and insetting small elements piece by piece. Bird construction calls for a multiplicity of small parts. This peculiarity lends itself to assembly on the pattern. If parts have been bevel-cut the bird's outline is likely to be slightly increased. It is not unusual for the completed bird to bulge slightly beyond pattern line. For better joints it is advisable to remove the completed bird assembly from the pattern and keep it under weights for overnight before continuing the work.

To set a completed bird into a background, place the bird on the back of the background veneer, with the bird's good side down. Tape bird to veneer with 3/4" masking tape to keep it from sliding. Slowly mark around the bird's outline with your knife, removing and replacing tape as encountered. Taping the bird to the background is a critical point in the technique. The outline usually is long and complex. Cutting is exacting work. Any slight movement of the bird will result in a disastrously poor joint. Hold the knife almost perpendicular when cutting out the background. Omit virtually all bevel in the cut. This practice makes the best inlay. When the cut is finished set the bird into the window from the front. Rub glue quickly into the joints from the back. Tape the inset in place on the back. Sand the front promptly. Sawdust fills the glue-fresh joints. Remove excess glue. Follow recommended finishing methods for marquetry pictures.

Albert C. Parker

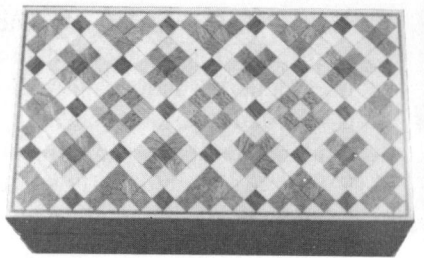

16. Parquetry designs and methods

The technique of combining geometric wood pieces into flat surface decoration is very old. The early Egyptians were masters of the art. French furniture makers incorporated parquetry in elaborate ways in their fancy furniture. Most of us today think first of wood floors when the term is mentioned. To relate the art of parquetry to this book we will define it as the art of geometric marquetry.

Parquetry procedure borrows some of marquetry's methods but limits itself to straight cuts. Veneers are cut into squares, triangles and diamonds. Usually the cut pieces are assembled into a sheet which is laid as a single piece on a flat wood surface. Large cut pieces intended to cover a table top or to decorate a sizable panel are sometimes laid individually to avoid the hazard of handling an oversize taped assembly of veneer pieces.

The primary tools for parquetry are a craft knife or a single-edge razor blade, a steel

An endless variety of intricate designs can be formed with sections cut out of a checkerboard assembly of two or more contrasting veneers

straightedge and an assortment of metal triangles providing 45, 60 and 30 degree corners. If you cannot buy suitable triangles cut them from sheet metal. Six-inch triangles are handiest and are large enough for most work. You need a 90-degree steel square and a simple bench hook such as the one in Chapter 18 designed for cutting fillets and borders.

The best veneers for parquetry are those having straight grain. A parquetry pattern is inherently busy and would become bizarre if composed of veneers having wild or strongly irregular figure. In general a selection of only two or three color tones — light, medium and dark — will work best.

For your first parquetry experiment it is best to start with a simple design of squares such as those required for a chessboard. The next easy step to try is to cut triangles. Gradually you will find ways of creating interesting design patterns by alternating the grain direction of every other veneer strip in an assembly of two-color strips, or by turning over every other strip, or shifting every other strip by a distance of one square to left or right. Cutting an assembly of squares on diagonals and varying the cutting angles can produce some wholly unexpected results. The possibilities are endless. If you enjoy simple parquetry you will want to experiment with more complicated switches of cuts and variations of assembly.

The method used for making a chessboard is a basic method for making many parquetry patterns. Start with one sheet each of light and dark veneer, each measuring at least 9" x 17". Place one sheet against the

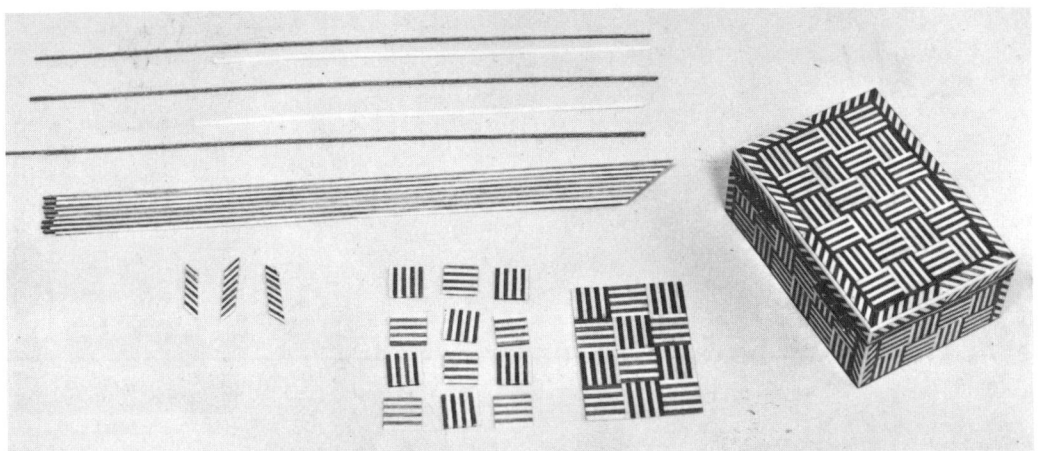

16-1. Checker design made of contrasting strips of veneer edge-glued, cut square and at an angle

edge of the bench hook. Lay a 2-inch straightedge on top and cut a strip. Continue cutting to accumulate four strips 2" wide by 17" long. Cut four strips of dark and four strips of light. Tape the strips together, alternating colors. With the 90-degree square, trim one end, making it square with an adjoining edge. Lay the trimmed end against the bench hook. Lay your straightedge on top and cut strips 2" wide. You now have eight assembled strips composed of alternating 2" squares. Turn every other strip end for end and tape them to create a complete chessboard assembly of 2-inch squares alternating light and dark.

You can utilize the chessboard principle for making a small marquetry lay-on to cover the lid of a readymade craft box. Cut narrow strips, 1/4" or less, of light and dark veneer. Follow all steps in the chessboard example. Then you can cut up the final veneer assembly in any number of ways to produce patterned sections which you combine into an overall design. Cutting the assembly on the diagonal will yield triangles and diamonds. With practice you will be able to

create intricate patterns like those illustrated.

There are other cutting and assembly methods. Instead of making a primary assembly of even squares you can cut long thin strips of light and dark veneer. (16-1) Edge-glue the strips and cut the assembly into squares for the central portion of a box lid. Turn adjoining squares to form a checkered design. Cut the assembly of strips at an angle and you have a diagonally patterned border.

One marquetarian who has developed the art of parquetry to a high level uses a small powered hand grinder for cutting strips. A table complete with fence and miter gauge was built around the power tool which is fitted with a tiny saw blade. (16-2) Dark and light veneer strips are cut 1/16" wide on the saw and assembled alternately. This assembly is then passed through the saw at a 45-degree angle (16-3) to produce border strips having a diagonal pattern.

16-2. Below, homemade mini saw slices veneer into thin strips. 16-3 right, shows assembly of edge-glued strips being angle-cut for border

17. Decorating boxes with veneer designs

Small boxes make welcome gifts when enriched with veneers. Most marquetarians have discovered this simple way to solve perplexing gift problems, and many beginning craftworkers make box veneering their first projects. Plain wood boxes in many shapes and sizes are available for desk use, jewelry, savings bonds, kitchen recipes, buttons and needles, musical units, cards and chips, household kitty money and other safe-keeping personal requirements. You can make your own boxes to specifications or you can buy unfinished boxes in craft supply stores.

Ordinarily the choice of design is influenced by the end purpose of the box. Veneer with small figure is preferable because of the small surfaces being covered. And small designs look better than large patterns on a small surface.

Standard marquetry techniques are used for preparing patterns, cutting and assembling veneer parts, mounting and finishing. The first step is removal of hinges and other hardware that may have come on the box. Next, tape the lid to the box. Trace the outline of ends, back, front and lid on paper. Develop your marquetry design for each area. Some designs require the making of lid and compartment side panels separately. Veneer sheets without marquetry designs can be laid over an entire side panel. In this method consider each of the outlines as one

Geometric marquetry assembly goes on lid of a readymade unfinished box. Strips for sides of lid and compartment are cut and glued on separately

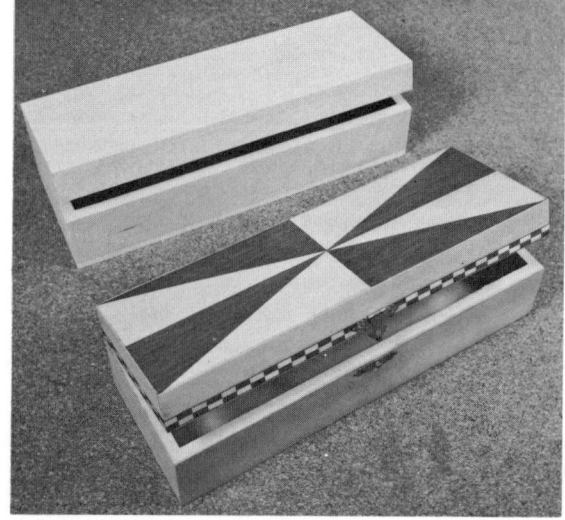

At left, rose design for box lid is developed by using pattern and window method of insetting veneer parts into overall veneer background. Initialed box below holds tiny musical unit and has space for jewelry. Curly maple was laid on all panels. Initialed walnut disc was inset

piece. The end outline, for example, is the pattern for the entire end and will be laid as one piece of veneer. Later a cut will be made in the veneer to separate lid from compartment. Add about 1/16" to each pattern edge to provide for overlap. Glue on the end pieces first. When the glue is dry trim overhang with a veneer saw. Then use a straightedge to locate the meeting line so you can cut along this line to separate lid from compartment. Cut with a craft knife or single-edge razor blade. Again align lid and compart-

ment and secure with tape. Glue on the front and back panels next. Lightly sand all surfaces before applying the top panel.

You may have to vary the described veneering procedure to meet special requirements of your design or marquetry assemblies. Some craftworkers lay veneer first on the back, then the sides, front and top to hide as many edges as possible when the box is viewed from front and above. A square of felt may be glued to the bottom. Fabric is sometimes glued to interior surfaces. If the interior is to be painted this should be done first. Exterior surfaces are masked with paper and tape. If you elect to veneer edges this should be done before any other veneering. Patterns must then be enlarged to accommodate the extra height of panels.

Intricate marquetry assembly applied to large box demonstrates high level of patience and skill. Two smaller boxes show mixed assemblies of two veneer sheets saw-cut at one time. This dual cutting is generally called Boulle work

127

18. Useful inventions and innovations

King-size fret saws. The confidence that comes with acquired skill in handling a fret saw inevitably leads to a desire to make larger and larger pictures. Commercial fret saws, the largest of which has a 12-inch throat, restrict you to sizes of pictures measuring less than 12 inches on the diagonal or require stopping the saw to make a new insertion point for the blade to let the saw frame swing around a corner of the workpiece. The problem is solved by making your own fret saw larger than you can buy. Two models are illustrated. The larger one was made from a length of steel gas line bought at an auto supply store. The smaller one was made from a length of aluminum channel located at a shop that makes aluminum windows and screens. The fittings—two chucks and a handle—were taken from smaller fret saws bought just for the purpose of providing the proper fittings. Although the large frames are lightweight, their excessive length exerts a slight downward drag which must be compensated for by a slight forward tilt with the cutting hand to counterbalance the drag.

Making large veneer sheets. Veneers come to you in widths from 4" up depending upon the tree size of the species. When you need a sheet of exotic veneer wider than anything in your stockpile you can build the size you require. The joint you make will be inconspicuous, in fact virtually invisible, if you follow this method. Overlap two sheets lengthwise with about 1/4" of the top sheet extending over the long edge of the bottom sheet. Guide your veneer saw along a steel straightedge to make a saw cut through both pieces without shifting veneer or straightedge. One clean saw cut should trim about 1/8" from the edge of each sheet. Assemble the two cut edges together tightly, binding them with a strip of veneer tape. Roller hard. Rollering is the way to make paper tape stick well. Next, turn the assembly over, flex ever so slightly to open the joint. Run white glue into the open joint from end to end. A little smearing won't hurt anything because this is the side to be glued later to a mounting panel.

Sealing open grain. Woods such as rosewood and teak should be sealed. One good way is to apply multiple thin coats of the

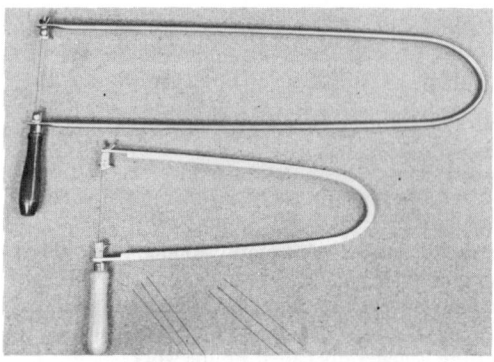

final finishing material you have decided on. Let each coat dry thoroughly before sanding and applying the next coat. Use a sanding block. Sand lightly and evenly. After a few thin coats if hollows due to the very open grain are still evident, use fine steel wool to get into the hollows so the next coat will fill in and adhere better.

Sizing veneer. To make brittle veneer more flexible and stronger you could try sizing it before attempting to cut or mount it. Mix a solution as follows:
Cascamite Resin Powder—2 measures
Flour—1 measure
Water—3 measures
Alcohol—1/2 to 1 measure

The solution should be used cold. Provide a suitable trough or vat which is large enough for veneers to be completely immersed for a minute or two. When you take them out of solution stand them on end to drain. As soon as the surface becomes dry to the touch lay each sheet separately between dry softwood caul boards which have been warmed. Basswood and poplar are good choices. Place weights on the top caul to keep the veneers flat. After twenty-four hours transfer veneers to another set of dry caul boards. In this manner the veneers dry and shrink slowly. At the end of the treatment the veneers should be flat, stronger, more flexible and less likely to split when being worked. Cutting, jointing and mounting are now easier.

Sanding open grain. When sanding a completed marquetry picture, sand in the direction of the grain of the major part of the picture. Keep at least three-quarters of the sanding block on the face of the picture to avoid rounding the edges. Do not use short strokes or circular motion. When sanding open-grain woods such as oak, sand at a slight angle to the grain. If you sand with the grain you may enlarge the pores of the wood. Sanding at an angle will level the high spots easier and quicker.

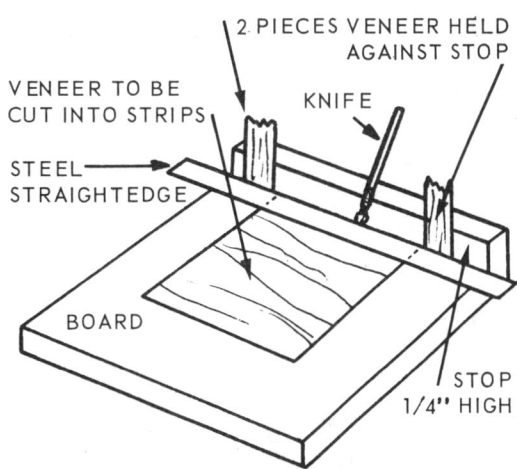

Stringer cutting jig. Narrow strips of veneer are needed in uniform width for stringers that surround a picture. Strips no thicker than veneer are used in fragmentation. Cutting a quantity of strips of the same width can be simplified by a universal jig developed for cutting multiple pieces of just about any width you want. It's very easy to assemble. Attach a backstop to a cutting board. Locate two scraps of veneer or wood of the exact thickness of required strips. Tape these filler pieces to the backstop if desired. Slip a sheet of chosen veneer between the fillers and against the backstop. On top of the veneer lay your steel straightedge. Cut with a craft knife.

Shellac for marquetry. When properly thinned, shellac makes a good undercoat for varnish or lacquer. It seals well and provides a hard transparent undercoat. Shellac is acceptable as a final coat on pictures, usually topped with wax, but not as a final coat on marquetry lay-ons applied to boxes, trays or table tops where a working surface is involved.

When buying shellac keep these points in mind. The natural color of shellac is orange, but most people buy white. Orange should be applied only on dark woods as it will darken light woods and probably show lap marks. White shellac contains a bleaching agent which shortens its shelf life to about six to twelve months. Be sure to look for a date stamped on the container of white shellac. Do not buy old shellac. And do not use out-dated shellac which you have on hand. Do not apply in hot or humid weather. It is apt to turn milky. Do not put hot items on a shellac finish. Shellac is not waterproof and not alcohol-proof.

Template for circles. Cutting a circle in veneer background to make a window for an insert is easier when you use a template. Empty plastic containers for food and pills collect fast around home. They are available in just about any size you could want for marquetry. Use the bottles as templates for guiding your craft knife when making an incised trackline on veneer. With the bottle removed the trackline remains as a groove for the knife to follow.

Varnish-can film. Before starting to finish a picture pour the approximate amount of finish needed into a separate receptacle, and before replacing the cover on the can clean out the rim with a cloth. Put enough clean marbles or smooth, clean pebbles into the can to bring the surface of the liquid to the top of the can. This practice eliminates air space and helps to stop the formation of film. After each use add more marbles. When the can is empty drop marbles into thinner so they will be ready for the next time.

Glue sealer. When your picture is ready for mounting don't forget to apply a good sealer on the back of the veneer assembly. This application helps to prevent contact cement from seeping through joints and causing trouble with your finish. A coat of water-thinned white glue or alcohol-thinned shellac should be used.

Removing rubber cement. Fret-saw and scroll-saw cutting methods sometimes require a pattern to be cemented to the piece of veneer you wish to cut. This is often done for replacement parts. The customary adhesive is rubber cement. It allows easy removal of the pattern after the cutting has been accomplished. The pattern pulls right off, but the cement may be stubborn. Usually you can ball up the cement under your fingertips. By forming the cement bits into a larger ball you can provide yourself with a pick-up device that hastens the removal job. Occasionally rubber cement will stain the wood. This happens to purpleheart regularly. The best defense is to use rubber cement only on waste areas of the pattern, outside the piece you wish to keep.

Knife blades for veneer. No. 11 surgical blades are excellent for cutting veneer. They are tapered and sharply pointed. Be sure to have the proper handle to hold these super-sharp blades. The standard type of handle has a knurled chuck. If the chuck has a tendency to loosen after prolonged use, wrap a short length of masking tape around the knurling. This addition also reduces finger blisters that come from continual cutting.

Warped veneer. To flatten badly warped and buckled veneer first dampen the piece evenly on both sides. Do not soak. Allow time for moisture to penetrate the sheet of veneer before you place it between cauls. Veneer is elastic if allowed to flatten slowly, but brittle if heavily weighted too rapidly. Weights, therefore, should be added a little at a time to give the veneer a chance to conform and settle itself into the new shape you are imposing. Only when the sheet is almost flat and when the moisture content is almost normal should the last weights be applied or clamps fully tightened. By trying to hasten this procedure—adding weights too fast— you will find that the veneer will return to its warped state. Use only enough pressure to bring the veneer flat in order that normal shrinkage can take effect gradually. It is advisable to keep flattened veneer under weights until you are ready to use it.

Hairline cracks in veneer. Small hairline cracks may be closed by carefully applying a few drops of water to the immediate area and pressing the sides together. This should be done prior to mounting and before any finish is applied.

Veneer trimmer. You can make this handy marquetry tool for a few cents. It is a veneer trimmer that is used to remove overhanging veneer from your picture. It also can be used to cut narrow border stringers for pictures. The simple tool consists of a small block of wood and a single-edge razor blade. The bottom edge of the block is curved. The blade is fastened to the block with machine screws for easy replacement. When trimming irregular grain or hard veneers you should make several passes over the veneer. The curved lower edge of the tool can be rocked a little more with each pass. This movement lowers the tip of the blade deeper into the veneer. Change blades frequently. To improve your metal straightedge, glue a strip of medium sandpaper on the underside and it will hold its position without slipping.

Protect light woods. After your picture has been mounted, but before it is sanded, brush on a wash coat of one part fresh shellac mixed with three parts alcohol. Allow to dry thoroughly. This coat fills pores and fine cracks. It prevents sanding dust of darker woods from getting into the grain of lighter woods during subsequent sanding.

Padding veneers. Double-sided adhesive tape with protective backing on one side may be used to hold pieces of veneer together in a sandwich or pad. Tape is applied to one piece of veneer and pressed down with a roller. Paper backing is then peeled off and the second piece of veneer is pressed onto the exposed adhesive side of the tape. After the pad has been cut into picture elements the pieces of veneer can be separated carefully with a dull kitchen knife. The tape remaining on the veneer is then removed by balling up with your fingertips.

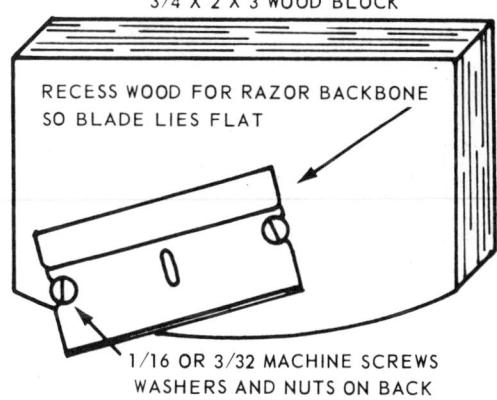

3/4 X 2 X 3 WOOD BLOCK

RECESS WOOD FOR RAZOR BACKBONE SO BLADE LIES FLAT

1/16 OR 3/32 MACHINE SCREWS WASHERS AND NUTS ON BACK

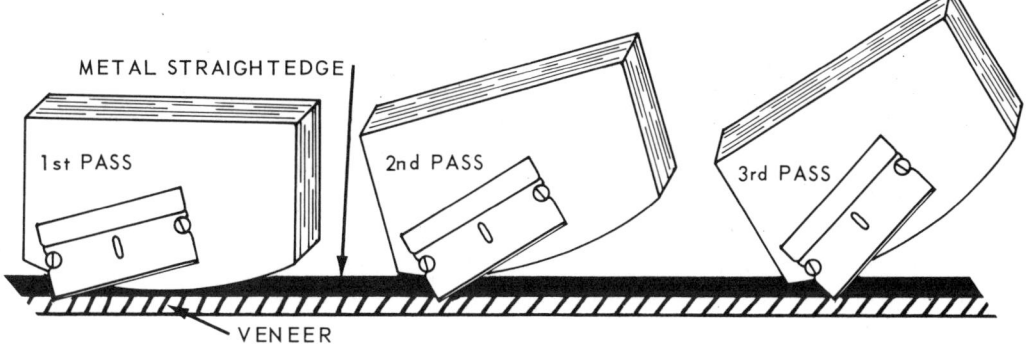

METAL STRAIGHTEDGE

1st PASS

2nd PASS

3rd PASS

VENEER

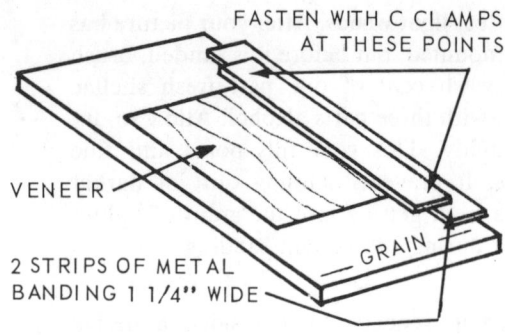

FASTEN WITH C CLAMPS
AT THESE POINTS

VENEER

2 STRIPS OF METAL
BANDING 1 1/4" WIDE

GRAIN

Cutting guide. Various setups are used for cutting duplicate veneer strips to uniform width. One method utilizes two long metal bars which have been edge-filed to precision. The bars are clamped to a cutting board. The bottom bar acts as a backstop for veneer, while the top bar establishes the width of the strip and serves as a metal straightedge for guiding knife or veneer saw.

Edge-glued assemblies. If you edge-glue veneer pieces as you cut and assemble them be sure to wipe off excess glue from the surface of the veneer. Use a damp cloth, not wet. Any glue left on the surface will prevent finishing materials from getting to the wood surface. Glue causes a glazing effect and will be noticeable in your final finish.

Extraordinary veneers. Unusual effects often can be achieved by making your own veneer from fallen fence posts, discarded parts of broken furniture, implements, and pruned limbs of lilac, pussywillow and shrubbery. After the wood has dried sufficiently slice it veneer-thin on a table saw. Be prepared for unusual colors and figures.

Restoring. After a picture has been hanging for a considerable time glue lines have been known to rise above the surface. This condition is a chemical reaction between glue and finishing material. Remove the line by rubbing the surface with 400 or 500 finishing paper. Follow by a light rubbing with 4/0 steel wool. Polish with rottenstone and oil. By exercising care you can avoid a complete refinishing job.

Brush keeper. Make a short-term brush keeper for finishing and adhesive brushes. Clean a one-pound coffee can. Cut a slit at the center of the plastic lid for the brush handle to slip through and form a tight fit. Pour solvent in the can. Replace the lid. Adjust the brush so it enters the solvent but does not rest on the bottom of the can.

Matching filler. Save sawdust from veneers. Keep it in labeled plastic pill bottles. When you need filler for a specific veneer simply mix the matching sawdust with white glue to form paste filler.

Leveling veneer. If necessary to use a piece of veneer that varies in thickness keep the side that will be the face of the picture as flat as possible. Cover the entire face with veneer tape. This covering gives enough support so rough sandpaper can be used on the back to level all high spots before gluing to a panel.

Blade sharpener. A handy sharpening device for the worktable consists of a wooden paddle covered on two sides as indicated in the drawing. In use, draw the blade of your marquetry knife along the emery face. Press it down as you draw it. The reverse side is a leather strop pierced with a pin to make hundreds of tiny holes into which polishing rouge is rubbed. Finish sharpening the blade by stropping. This little accessory assures cleaner cuts in veneer and longer-lasting blades.

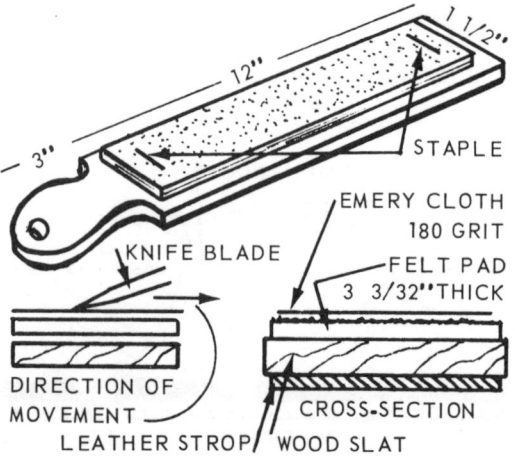

12"

1 1/2"

3"

STAPLE

KNIFE BLADE

EMERY CLOTH
180 GRIT

FELT PAD
3 3/32" THICK

DIRECTION OF
MOVEMENT

CROSS-SECTION

LEATHER STROP

WOOD SLAT

1

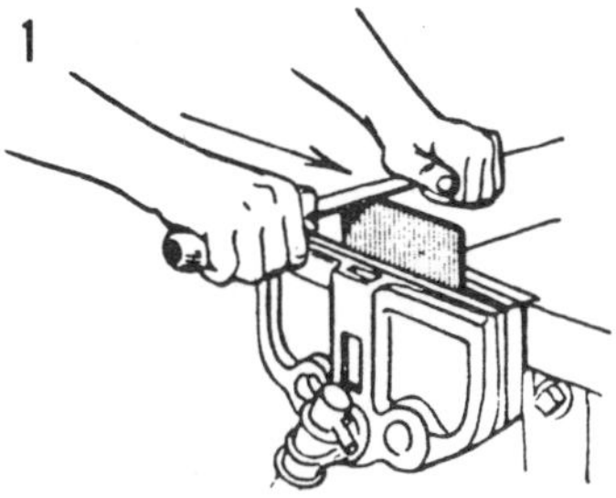

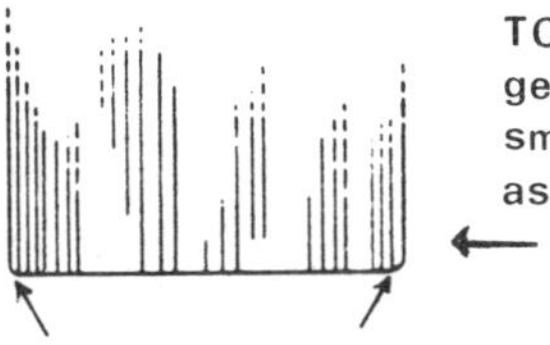

TO SHARPEN THE HAND SCRAPER: File the edges square and straight by drawfiling with a smooth mill file. Round the corners slightly, as shown.

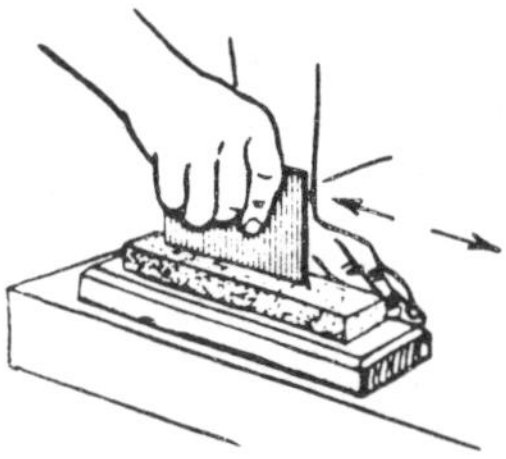

2

Whet the edge, holding the blade square to the surface of the oilstone. Some prefer to hold the scraper square to the edge of the oilstone.

3

Remove the burr by whetting the scraper flat on the oilstone. The edges should be very smooth and sharp.

4

Draw the edge with three or four firm strokes of the burnisher held flat on the scraper.

5

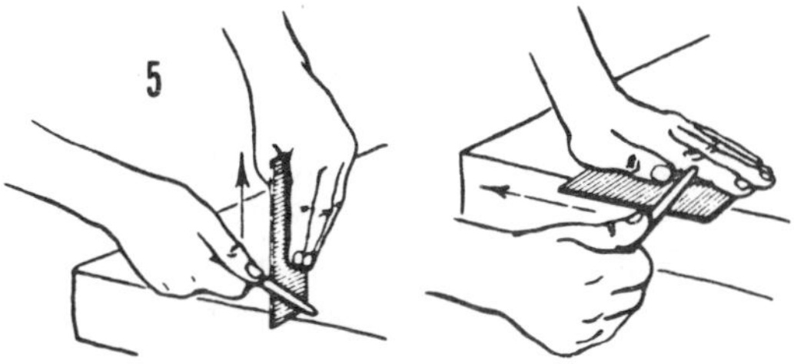

Turn the edge with a few strokes of the burnisher. The scraper can be held in either of the two ways. Draw the burnisher toward you the full length of the blade, with a sliding stroke.

6

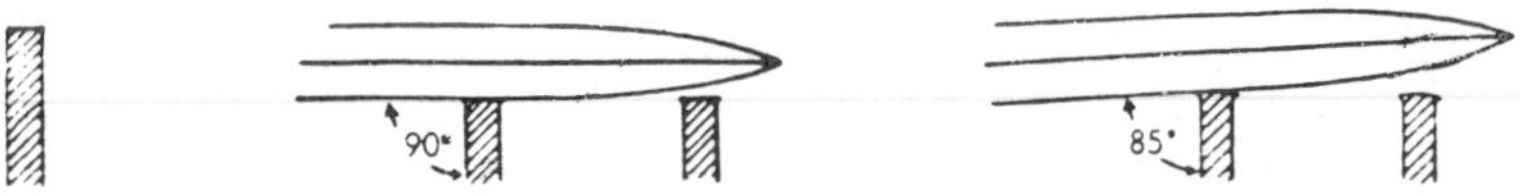

90°   85°

To turn the edges out the burnisher is held at 90 degrees to the face of the blade for the first stroke. For each of the following strokes, tilt the burnisher slightly until at the last stroke it is held at about 85 degrees to the face of the blade. A drop of oil on the burnisher helps.

7

The hand scraper can be either pushed or pulled as the grain of the wood demands or whichever is more convenient.

The hand scraper is held firmly between the thumb and fingers at an angle of about 75 degrees and sprung to a slight curve by pressure of the thumbs. Dust, instead of a shaving indicates a dull scraper.

8

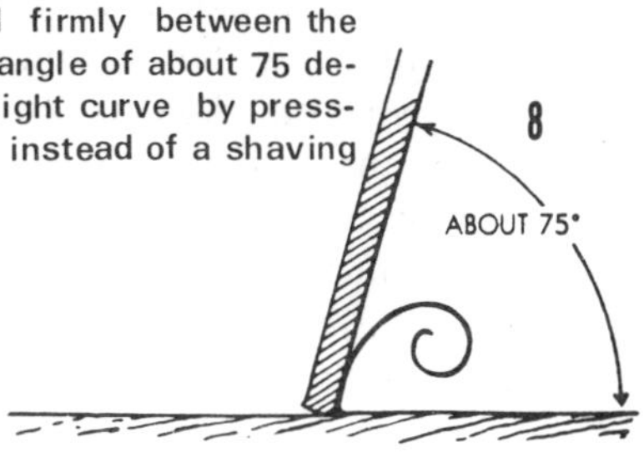

ABOUT 75°

Blade threading fixture. Many advanced marquetarians have simplified the blade threading problem with a homemade device. Basically the fixture is a typical bird's-mouth saw table V-notched at one end. From the vertex of the V-notch a 1/8 slot is cut to a depth of 3 inches. The saw table is mounted on the upper edge of a centerboard. At the front edge of this centerboard two tool clips are attached. When you make this device be sure to size it to fit your fret saw. Buy tool clips that fit your style of handle.

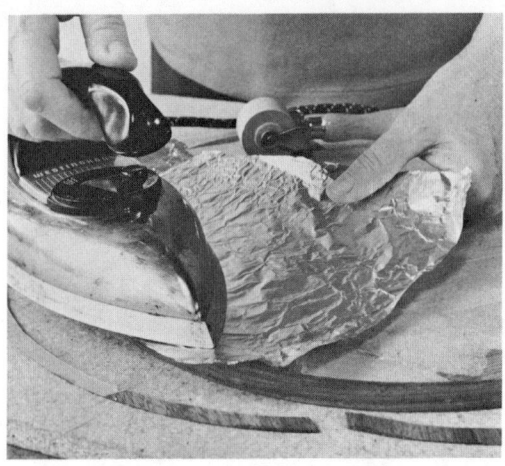

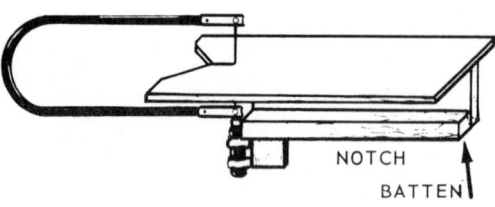

NOTCH
BATTEN

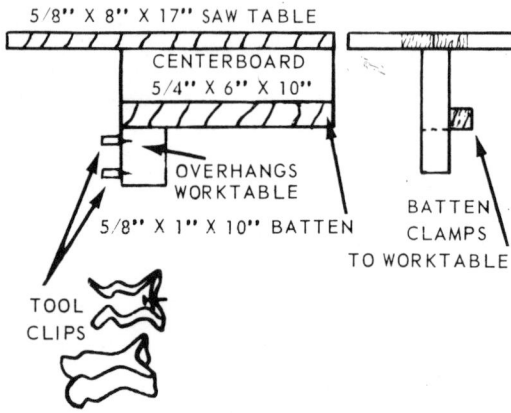

5/8" X 8" X 17" SAW TABLE

CENTERBOARD
5/4" X 6" X 10"

OVERHANGS
WORKTABLE

5/8" X 1" X 10" BATTEN

BATTEN
CLAMPS
TO WORKTABLE

TOOL
CLIPS

To thread the blade push the saw handle into the two clips. Pass the blade about half-way through the needle hole in the veneer. Lock the lower end of the blade in the chuck, then lock the upper end while squeezing the frame enough for blade tension. Pull away from the clips and start sawing in the V-notch. If your method is bevel-cutting, notch, slot and upper edge of the center-board can be cut at a 12-degree angle. If you use a full centerboard, clamp it in a bench vise for use. A notched centerboard can be clamped to your worktable.

Laying down blisters. There are various reasons for blisters occurring on veneer faces or backs. One cause is too much moisture applied to peel off veneer facing tape in a hurry. Lay the blister back down with heat from an electric iron set at moderate heat. Hold aluminum foil between iron and veneer. Heat drives moisture from the veneer and softens underneath glue at the same time. Roller the area hard. Repeat this treatment if necessary, then clamp the area between caul boards for a few hours.

Knife-cutter's board. A tilted cutting board reduces arm fatigue and improves visibility. Users say that it is easier to see fine pattern lines on veneer when the veneer is slightly raised. The simplest cutting board consists of two pieces of hardboard fastened together along one short end with small hinges. The upper panel is supported at any convenient angle by a block of wood slipped between the two panels. Remove the block, and the cutting board stores flat in very little space.

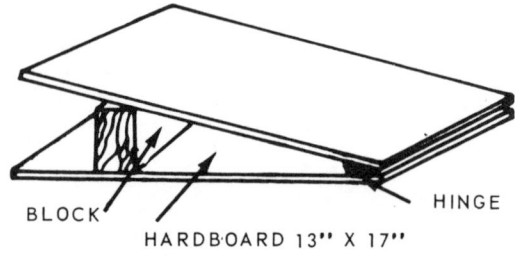

BLOCK

HINGE

HARDBOARD 13" X 17"

Edge splintering. To reduce the possibility of edge splintering it is a good practice to break, or round, all veneer edges very slightly with sandpaper. This should be done before you apply finish of any kind.

Picture sources. Subjects for marquetry pictures abound in libraries, art stores and gift shops. Look for ideas in books, magazines, greeting cards, postcards, photographs, slides, children's coloring books, painting and drawing books, and needlecraft designs.

Picture preview. To see how your unfinished veneer picture will look after it has been varnished wipe the veneers with turpentine. This treatment brings out the wood colors remarkably. Afterwards, be sure to allow drying time before sanding and applying varnish.

Water sprayer. An empty "Windex" bottle with its finger-pumped plunger makes an excellent device for spraying a controlled amount of water on veneers that are about to be flattened under weights.

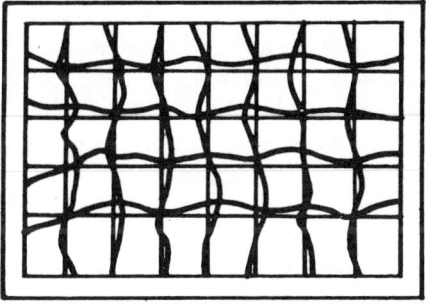

Using scraps. When leftover odd shapes of veneer accumulate to a point where you must find a use or discard them, try making a crazy quilt backing on a mounting panel. On the back of the panel draw border lines. Fill in the remaining area with horizontal and vertical crossing lines to form a grid. Scribe zigzag lines following more or less the grid pattern. Cut and fit veneer scraps to fill the irregular areas. Edge-glue as you assemble. Mix colors and figure of adjoining pieces to make a lively crazy quilt pattern to show your friends.

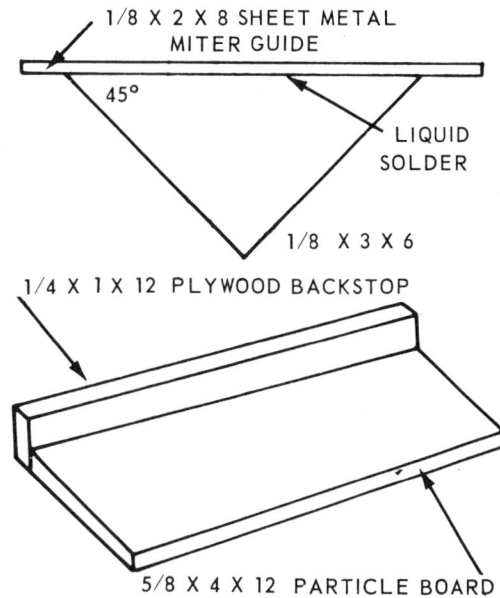

1/8 X 2 X 8 SHEET METAL MITER GUIDE

45°

LIQUID SOLDER

1/8 X 3 X 6

1/4 X 1 X 12 PLYWOOD BACKSTOP

5/8 X 4 X 12 PARTICLE BOARD

Miter guide for knife. Veneer strips being prepared to form a border around a marquetry picture are usually mitered on the mounting board. Strips are cut long enough to overlap meeting strips. Both strips are cut at one time to form a close miter. Some workers say they prefer to cut miters separately with a guide. One simple type of guide is illustrated for you to make. The guide itself is a triangle of sheet metal attached with solder to a metal backbone which stands on a long edge. A cutting board has a backstop attached to one edge. Veneer is laid on the cutting board. The metal guide is held on top of the veneer where one of its 45-degree sides will rest at desired miter location. Your craft knife rides against the guide. The device is especially useful when parquetry designs with many diagonal edges are being developed.

Sealer coat. As an excellent substitute for commercially prepared sealers you can compound your own sealer by mixing one part fresh shellac with three parts of alcohol. Wait for the sealer coat to dry thoroughly before lightly sanding the surface. Always clean sanding dust from a surface before applying other finishing coats. Most experienced wood finishers use a vacuum brush and a tack cloth for cleaning.

Trimming circular plaques. To cut edging overhang from circular plaques without breaking it hold the plaque upright and roll it slowly as you cut off the trim. Keep knife point moving at the same speed so that the overhang at point of knife is resting on cutting board. At the same time exert some downward pressure on the plaque.

Fixed width guides. One of the simplest cutting guides for fixed width strips needed as borders or edging for mounting panels consists of a plain cutting board without attachments. Used with it is a length of angle

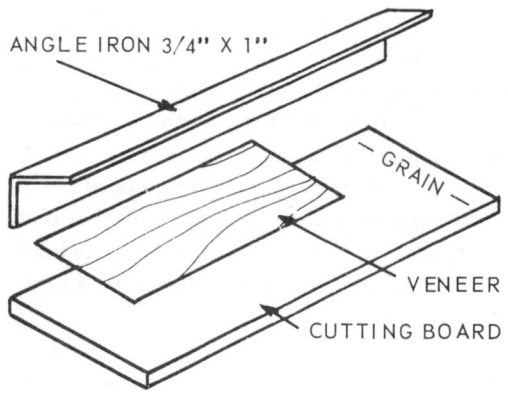

ANGLE IRON 3/4" X 1"

GRAIN

VENEER

CUTTING BOARD

iron which hooks over the back edge of the board. The so-called leg dimensions of the angle iron determine the widths of strips you can cut with this setup. Lay veneer on the cutting board, apply hand pressure on the angle iron to hold down the veneer. The front edge of the angle iron serves as a straightedge for your cutting tool. Another version of cutting guide is made by attaching a backstop at the back edge of a cutting board and using a straightedge as both a cutting guide and a width gauge.

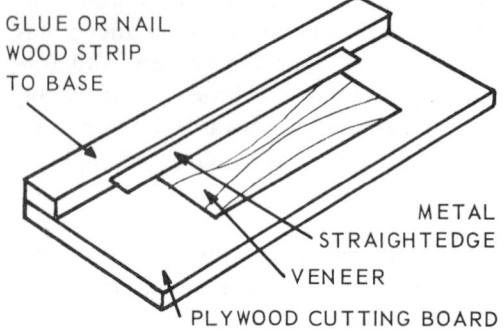

GLUE OR NAIL
WOOD STRIP
TO BASE

METAL
STRAIGHTEDGE

VENEER

PLYWOOD CUTTING BOARD

Well done. You have heard and perhaps used the expression, "that's good enough." It may be an excusable attitude in some activities but not in marquetry. Here, the end product of your craftsmanship remains on display for a very long time as the testimony of your ability. While you are working on a marquetry creation, and while there is still time for improvement, take the trouble to make over any part that is not the best you can produce.

19. Questions and answers about marquetry procedure

Q. What can be done to prevent warping when flakeboard is used for mounting a marquetry picture?

A. Whether you use flakeboard, plywood or tempered hardboard for mounting, a veneer backing should be used. This balances the stress. It also is advisable to apply sealer to the mounting board before gluing on the facing and backing. After mounting place the assembly in a press or under weights and allow the glue to dry thoroughly.

Q. What can be done to repair a veneer area that has accidentally been dented?

A. Gently sand off the finish over the dented area, place a drop of water on the area and let it stand overnight. Moisture raises the dent enough to sand it flat again. Afterwards apply finish to entire area.

Q. Sometimes a knife sticks while cutting veneers. Can this be prevented?

A. Coat the point of the knife by inserting the tip into a wax candle or a piece of wax. Also reduce your pressure on the knife. A sharp knife is essential for cutting veneer and it cuts best by using a series of light cuts rather than a heavy cut. Light cuts produce a cleaner cut.

Q. In the case of oily veneers what should be done to make them stick to the baseboard better?

A. Here you have several options. One is to use a sharp knife held at an angle of approximately thirty degrees. Slice the back side of the veneer face, making long flaps. The glue can then get under these flaps to form a better bond with the baseboard. Be exceptionally careful not to slice too deep, because the treatment might show through on the veneer face. Another way is to spread glue on the surface of the baseboard. While glue is tacking wash entire back of the face veneer with lacquer thinner even though the whole picture may not be of oily veneers. Then as quickly as possible lay the face veneer onto the baseboard and put the assembly into a press or under weights to dry.

Q. Sometimes after my marquetry pictures have been completed, I find hollows have formed between the veneer pieces. What is the cause and cure?

A. If you are using a water soluble contact adhesive it could cause shrinking and buckling. Use a non-water-base contact adhesive. When laying the veneer be sure to roller all pieces of veneer firmly from the center to the edge so that all air spaces are rolled out. To fill in the cracks make sawdust of the veneer by scraping a scrap piece of it with a knife. Mix the sawdust with white glue and fill in the cracks. Allow to dry and proceed with finishing.

Q. How can I cut burls without having them crack or chip at edges?

A. Tape the part of the burl to be cut. Use veneer tape preferably on both sides. Tape prevents chipping and cracking while the veneer is being cut. Don't remove tape until ready to glue or finish. Be sure to use several strokes of the knife rather than trying to cut through in one pass of the knife.

Q. What are the accepted principles for choosing veneers for a marquetry picture?

A. The choice is really an individual one. Generally it is advisable to use as little dyed veneers as possible. Let the beauty of natural veneers enhance your work. Look through your veneer stockpile and select one that most closely resembles the background whether it is sky, ocean or a plain wall. The window method of cutting is most helpful in choosing the best veneer because this method gives one the opportunity to turn the veneer in all directions while looking through the background space you have just cut in your waste veneer. You can judge the best position of the veneer before you cut it. Changing the direction of the grain sometimes produces a much better effect. After cutting your chosen background veneer and taping or gluing it in place, go to the next largest area of the picture. Cut a window out of the waste veneer and view your next choice of veneer through the window, turning it in various directions as you did with the background piece. Continue on down to the smallest part. As your picture takes shape you will find it gets easier to choose veneers for detail work.

Q. Where is sand for sand shading obtained?

A. Pet shops, tropical fish stores and some paint dealers who stock anti-skid sand for floor paints. As a last resort get a pail and shovel and head for a clean beach.

Q. Where are cork sanding blocks sold?

A. Most hardware and paint stores.

Q. Where are non-skid rulers sold?

A. Art or draftsman supply stores.

Q. What would cause spotty adhesion and blistering of veneer when using contact cement?

A. Lack of adhesive on one or both sides of material to be bonded. While applying a first coat of cement, quickly rub it in well so that the adhesive comes into contact with all areas and does not leave any spot where the glue does not contact the wood. If the glue skips over a portion, this will probably form a bubble later on. When the first coat starts to appear glossy, in twenty to thirty minutes, apply a second coat. When both surfaces to be bonded are glossy and dry to the touch, line up the surfaces to be bonded and gradually make contact between the two, pressing out air bubbles as you go along. After the veneer is in place roller it from the center outward in all directions over and over again until you are quite sure all air bubbles have been pressed out. Lay a sheet of wax paper and a square of plywood over the face and place the assembly under weights or in clamps for several hours.

Q. Does the back side of a picture have to be level or will glue fill in the space?

A. The back side of a picture must be level before it is mounted. Carefully use rough sandpaper to reduce the high spots. Glue will not fill the different levels between picture and panel.

Q. What is the function of wallpaper sizing on veneers which are to be used in marquetry pictures and designs?

A. After a badly warped piece of veneer has been flattened by repeated dampening and drying under weights, apply a moderate coat of wallpaper size with a brush to the side that will be bonded. Cover with a piece of wax paper and place under weights until dry. In most instances the veneer will stay flat after this treatment.

Q. On prepared patterns what do the numbers stand for?

A. Originally the numbers referred to specific types of veneer sold by the supplier of the pattern. The two or three small parallel lines drawn near the number indicated the grain direction suggested for that particular piece of veneer. Substitutions of veneers are sometimes made by the manufacturer without notice being given to the purchaser. The numbers can be used as a basic guide, but a kit of identified veneer samples can be used as a more reliable guide to identification. These wood samples also serve as a source of supply for small missing veneers.

Q. What effect does sunlight have on a marquetry picture?

A. A marquetry picture containing dyed veneers is subject to fading. Dyed colors fade out of the base wood and leave a blotchy sycamore or whatever was originally dyed. The more intense the exposure to sunlight the faster the colors will disappear.

Q. Can a piece of furniture containing marquetry work be stained?

A. Yes. Assuming that there is no finish on either the furniture or the marquetry it is possible to stain the wood surrounding the marquetry by applying a sealer coat to the marquetry before applying stain. Be sure the base or solvent for the stain is not the same as that used for a sealer. Water stains and sanding sealer or a sealer coat of shellac are acceptable combinations. After stain has been allowed to dry a very light sanding is recommended for the entire piece prior to finishing.

Q. What is the best way for storing veneers?

A. The best way to store veneers is to keep them flat with the edges lined up as closely as possible. Cover with cardboard or plywood and place a weight on top. These precautions will minimize the danger of warping and splitting.

Q. How does one put a dollar value on his marquetry work when selling it?

A. When a marquetarian has created or copied a picture that appeals to him and has figured out what veneers to use and has finally completed the work, he has a picture that is an original and one that means a great deal to him. Try to put a price tag on that! The physical part of the endeavor is not too difficult to figure out in terms of hours worked, the cost of veneers and other materials. What you add to these basic factors is the intangible factor of what the picture is now worth to you. Price is a label you cannot establish solely by cost factors. Value is the worth of an item to you. When price and value equal each other, that is the ideal selling price.

Q. What would be the best veneers for a beginner to purchase?

A. In order to have both light and dark veneers to choose from, the beginner should get about eighteen to twenty-four varieties. Some of the most popular ones are sycamore, birch, avodire, maple, elm, walnut, padauk, sapele, lacewood, harewood, gaboon, gumwood, orientalwood, ash, beech, and burls of walnut, maple, ash and Carpathian elm. Keep in mind that veneers are not always identical. The same kind, purchased a few days apart, will come to you in variations of shade and figure.

Q. How can white-glue stain be removed from veneer?

A. According to the manufacturer "there is little that can be done once the glue has penetrated the wood." Staining may be prevented when the wood is clamped if excess glue is immediately wiped away with a damp cloth before it has a chance to penetrate the wood.

Q. What is the best way to remove pencil and carbon paper marks from the face of veneers?

A. Gentle scraping with a knife or single-edged razor blade. Sanding will only smear it into the wood deeper.

Q. Is it possible to replace a segment in a marquetry assembly after it has been mounted?

A. Yes. By careful use of your craft knife, cut around the outline of the segment to be removed. Cut through the veneers to the face of the mounting board. Using a small chisel or chisel-like cutting tool, remove the unwanted piece from within the outline. Exercise care not to cut into the good surrounding areas and do not cut into the mounting panel. When all the unwanted material has been removed lay a piece of thin white paper over the area where you have removed the veneer. Tape it so it will not move. Use a soft black pencil and hold it so the largest portion of the carbon point is in contact with the paper. Lightly rub the pencil back and forth over the area. You will soon see a sharp outline of the vacated area. Using rubber cement, glue the paper pattern on the new piece of veneer that you want to insert. Cut around the outer side of the outline. It is easier to remove veneer than add it. When you have the proper fit apply white or yellow glue in the hole and set your new piece in place. Wipe off excess glue. Cover with wax paper and clamp for overnight.

Q. Can veneers and marquetry be applied over metal surfaces?

A. Very easily. Since the development of modern contact adhesives and in particular veneer glue, veneers can be applied to almost any surface. A modern fad is to apply veneers and marquetry assemblies to the dash panels of automobiles.

Q. Can scratches be removed from a marquetry piece?

A. Usually light scratches on the surface do not penetrate the finish. Most such scratches can be removed by using polishing compound or pumice and oil or water. Scratches that penetrate into the veneer of the marquetry may require removal of the entire finish. A cabinet scraper does this well. It may be possible to swell the scratch in the veneer with a few drops of water, or you may elect to replace that damaged piece of veneer and then refinish the entire assembly.

Q. Can colors that have faded from veneers be rejuvenated?

A. Each case is an individual study. In most instances light scraping and sanding of the veneer surfaces will bring back the original tones. However, it is also possible that a piece may have been exposed to strong sunlight for a long period of time and the color may have faded away completely, in which case the only remedy is to replace the veneer.

Q. How many organizations are devoted to marquetry?

A. At the present time there are only two such known organizations—the British Marquetry Society and the Marquetry Society of America.

Index

Bibliography

Ancient Carpenter's Tools by Henry C. Mercer
The Art and Practice of Marquetry by William Alexander Lincoln
Encyclopedias: Americana, Britannica, International
Introducing Marquetry by Marie Campkin
Know Your Woods by Albert Constantine, Jr.
News Letter published by the Marquetry Society of America
Veneering Simplified and Veneer Craft for Everyone by Harry Jason Hobbs
The World of Leonardo da Vinci by Ivor B. Hart

Butternut

Teak

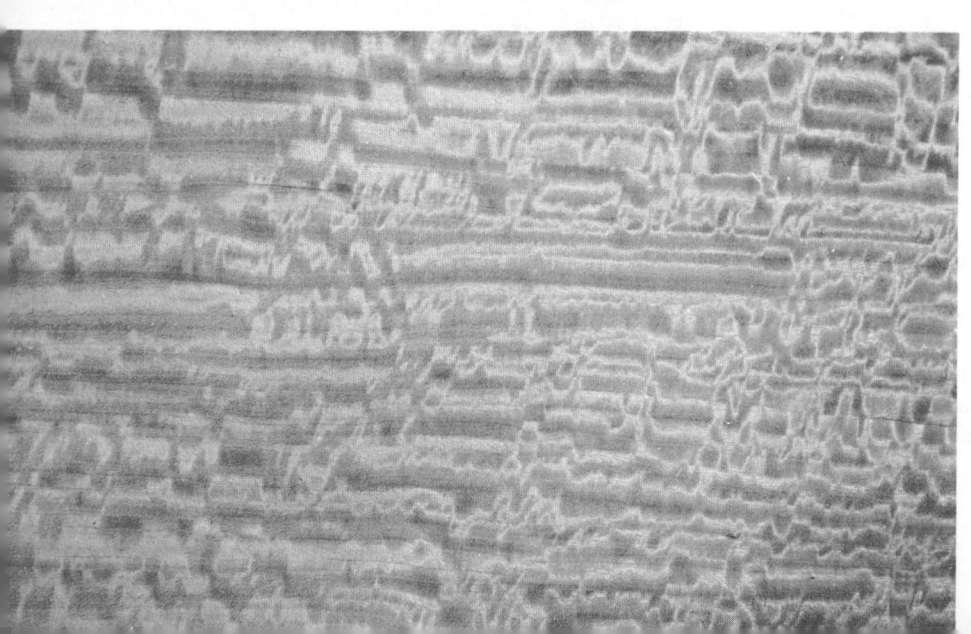

Satinwood bee's-wing